Mothers-in-Law Can Be Fun

LOU BEARDSLEY

HARVEST HOUSE PUBLISHERS
Eugene, Oregon 97402

MOTHERS-IN-LAW CAN BE FUN

This book is dedicated to
my precious in-law kids
(in order of their appearance)
Pattie, Jim, Dorene, and Debbie

Introduction

There are books on how to be happily married, raise our families, grow spiritually, balance our bank accounts, plan our meals, decorate our homes, take vacations, organize our time, care for our pets, and talk to our house plants. But I have never seen a book on how to be a mother-in-law. It's a totally surprising experience for most of us. We're busy raising children, keeping our husbands happy, and being good citizens when all of a sudden our son comes in with his adorable little cheerleader in tow and bashfully announces "We're engaged!" Or our daughter bursts into our bedroom at 2:00 A.M., sticks her left hand under our nose, and screeches "LOOK!" while her young man stands in the doorway trying not to look uncomfortable at seeing us in curlers and a wrinkled nightgown.

The next morning the realization hits us. Junior (or Sissy) is getting married! And we are forced into a new role—that dreaded, unfamiliar, butt-of-all-jokes title, "Mother-in-Law." We automatically have two strikes against us, and chances are that we have done no preparation for this new phase in the realm of parenthood. We have never sought counsel, read a book, been to a seminar, or taken a course on how to be an effective mother-in-law. We don't even have a job description! We're afraid to rush up to the couple with questions and advice for fear that they'll think we're going to be the interfering type. On the other hand, if we play it cool and adopt a "do-your-own-thing" attitude, they'll think we don't care and (heaven forbid) be closer to "that other family."

Oh, woe is us! How should we respond? How can we build a relationship that will last through the years and be close and warm and loving? How can we get to know this prospective member of the family? How do we continue to "mother" without "smothering," and put our babe out of the nest without putting him or her out of our lives? This book contains some answers based on God's Word, experience, and a survey taken by many married persons of all ages. The survey is included, and we suggest that you turn to the back of the book and fill it out before you read the following chapters. It will help you to see where your own mother-in-law has or hasn't failed, so that you can profit from her mistakes or example.

If you are much too young to be a mother-in-law, all the better. You can start preparing now to be the best one ever. If you are already a mother-in-law, there's nothing more helpful than some on-the-job training. It is a difficult assignment and the stakes are high. Your communications with your married children and their families to a great degree determines how happy you're going to be for the rest of your life. With the right balance of loving concern for them and involvement with your own interests, this "empty-nest" stage of life can be the most exciting of all. We pray that with God's help you will be able to implement the suggestions in this book into your life to enjoy your wedded offspring to the fullest.

CONTENTS

1

The Dating Game

Teenage Dating Period

Becoming a good mother-in-law is like learning to be a parent: it takes practice. Much of our success as parents comes from trial and error. Unfortunately, once we become mothers-in-law, the error part can have drastic results. God has provided us with a practice period, and that is during the time when our youngsters are dating. What better way to train for the future job of mother-in-law than on someone who will probably *not* be our child's lifetime mate?

Probably the best example of a mother-in-law in the Bible is that of Naomi, in the Book of Ruth. She was a mother-in-law under the most difficult of circumstances. Her sons and husband were dead, and her daughters-in-law were Moabites. This would be the modern-day equivalent of a Christian woman with two daughters-in-law who belonged to a cult. Naomi's husband had moved his family to this heathen country, where their two sons then married girls who were unbelievers.

I believe there is a lesson here for us: if it is necessary for us to move, it is of the utmost importance that we find a good, Bible-teaching church so that our children will have plenty of exposure to Christian young people. We should set standards for their dating, and one of those should be that they date only believers. This may seem strict and overly cautious, particularly when they are too young to have any thought of marriage. However, my next-door neighbor began dating her husband when they were both 14 years old. Most of us know high-school classmates who were a twosome at a young age and married upon graduation.

Only God can foresee how a relationship is going to turn out. That squeaky-voiced adolescent down the block who follows your daughter around may be your future son-in-law. If he is not a Christian, a problem is already in the making. He will either pull her away from her faith or cause her heartache in the years to come. The most unhappy women I've ever encountered are those who love the Lord but have husbands who do not share this love and may even be antagonistic toward it.

Naomi was the kind of mother-in-law every girl would want. Lange's commentary says, ''Ruth's confession of God and His people originated in the home of her married life. It sprang from the love with which she was permitted to embrace Israelites. . . . The conduct of one Israelite woman [Naomi] in a foreign land was able to call forth a love and a confession of God like that of Ruth. . . . Ruth loves a woman and is thereby led to the God whom that woman confesses.''

Naomi's actions and behavior toward her daughter-in-law were responsible for Ruth's conversion. All through the Book of Ruth we see Naomi's tender love for both of her daughters-in-law and her concern for their well-being. She wanted them to remarry and stay in their own country with their families. Orpah followed her advice, but Ruth loved her so deeply that she went with her to Judah. Undoubtedly Ruth could see the difference between Naomi, the woman of God, and the heathen women of her own people.

We as mothers-in-law should look to Naomi as an example to follow. Although the Bible doesn't go into much detail as to Naomi's conduct or specific actions, it does tell us how to treat other people. Jesus, by His words and example, gives us guidelines in living with and relating to others, and the epistles are full of instructions that amplify what He said. If we are in the Word and obedient to it, our in-law children should become as dear to us as our own offspring. Love begets love, and even though you may at this time have a strained relationship with one of your children's mates, God can change the situation. Luke 1:37 says, ''With God nothing is impossible.''

The starting point in a good relationship with an in-law is open communication and love between you and your own child. A rebellious child may marry someone unsuitable just to get even. Also, your child's mate will take on his feelings and attitudes toward you, so if there is bitterness between you and your own son or daughter, they will share it with their wife or husband.

If your children are in their teens (or younger), there are some guidelines for establishing good rapport with them. The first is, of course, to love them. You may hate some of the things they do, but always make sure that they are secure in the fact that they have your love to count on. Take their problems and their dates seriously. Remember that *they* do. Show them the same courtesy you would show a neighbor who comes to you for advice or sharing. It may seem like puppy love to you, but to your child, every dating relationship is a most serious thing. Teenagers have left home, quit school, or taken their own lives over something that their parents considered to be an adolescent "crush." Remember that all of us consider our own problems to be greater than those of others.

The second guideline in your relationship with your own child is prayer. Pray *for* them at least once a day, and pray *with* them once or twice each day. A good time to do this is when you awaken them in the morning. Arise a few minutes early and sit on the edge of their bed and pray for their day—for the Lord to lead and protect them, and if there is some special event or problem, pray for that too.

Pray with each child individually. You can do your group praying during the table grace, but each child needs time alone with you to pray about those needs that are special to him or her. A good time to pray with your child is while you are in the car alone with him. Keep your eyes open, of course, and just pray as you are driving along. If he comes to you with a problem or you have an argument with him, stop right then and pray about it. It is amazing how God can soothe hurt feelings and solve situations by softening hearts, both theirs and ours.

The third guideline is the establishment of rules and consistent discipline. Young people should know their parents' standards and what they expect of them. Once this has been established, punishment for willful disobedience should always be followed through. The teenager with no rules or guidelines is an unhappy one, with great insecurities. He doesn't know what is expected of him or even if his parents care what he does. If you have had good communication with your child over the years, he will know your standards, but it is still necessary to make them clear to him. Spell them out, and if an unusual situation arises, he will know from experience what you would have him do.

If your communication is less than good, there is no time like the present to start building it. The first thing to do is to ask his forgiveness for your lack of sensitivity and your failure to build the kind of relationship that God wants you to have. Tell him you would like to start now to have the kind of family that would glorify God so that you can enjoy each other through your lives and support each other during the trials that are sure to come. Admitting that you've been wrong is a humbling experience but one that will endear yourself to your child as he realizes that you too are human.

The families with the worst problems as their children grow up are those where the mother or father is a screamer or a nagger, or has a biting, sarcastic, critical tongue. One or the other is either a harsh disciplinarian without obvious love or else is completely permissive, never punishing for wrongdoing. The most maladjusted children seem to come from homes where the mother is over-critical and the father does not discipline. The children are devastated by the constant dispproval of their mother and made insecure by the role reversal in the family, in which the father is not the head of the household. If you see yourself in any of these situations, you have some serious work before you get your relationship with God, each other and your children into proper perspective. Counseling with a Christian pastor would be a good place to start. Pray for God's leading, and start immediately to rectify the situation.

Included in the back of this book is a survey in which to rate your mother-in-law. This was taken by women in a Bible class in Northern California, and the results were conclusive enough to influence the subject matter I have included in this book. One thing that impressed me most was how important the relationship that is established *before* the marriage is to the one which develops *after* the wedding day.

In question 33, ''How did your mother-in-law treat you when you were dating your mate? Warm and loving? Polite? Barely civil? Hostile?'' over half the women checked ''polite'' as their answer, rather than ''warm and loving.'' Now ''polite'' is better than ''barely civil'' or ''hostile,'' but the connotation is as you would treat a stranger, not a prospective member of the family. I am polite to someone to whom I have just been introduced and am not sure I will be meeting again. I am also polite to door-to-door salespeople, repairmen, bus drivers, delivery men, trash collectors, and store clerks. To everyone else I lean more toward the ''warm and loving'' category. I try to make friends of people I see often—the grocery clerks who wait on me week after week, the dentist, the doctor, the pharmacist, new people at church, neighbors, and my children's friends and their parents.

As for my children's dates, my husband and I have always tried to treat them warmly and lovingly, even if we were not completely in favor of the person. It has been more difficult when it was someone we felt would not be suited to our sons or daughter in marriage. Usually this was a case of not being mature spiritually or someone who obviously had severe problems in some area of his or her life. Our daughter once dated a young man from her Bible college who had real trouble submitting to authority. We tried to be warm and loving to him, but he was so defensive toward adults that he was unable to accept our offer of friendship. The relationship was terminated before it became serious, and we praised the Lord for that.

Another time, one of our sons dated a girl who

had very severe family problems and who was quite immature spiritually. We prayed that God would give us His love for her, and when we gave the whole situation to Him and treated her warmly, it was less than a month later that they broke off the relationship. Many of those whom our children dated still come to visit us periodically; in fact, we are like a second family to the young man who was once engaged to our daughter, and we look forward to his visits with his wife and son.

We have a home in the mountains to which we invited our children's dates (if they had reached the point of a "relationship"), and those times were very precious. A weekend together in the same house is a real help in finding out what a person is like, from the perspective of both sides. Many times, after a prolonged time together, our children would decide that the person they thought was so "neat" didn't really fit into the family. Mr. or Miss Wonderful turned out to be a picky eater or squeamish in the woods, or else did not enjoy a family time of games, singing around the big fire in the fireplace, or just sitting and talking.

If you don't own such a place, try renting one for a weekend or else going camping. We often did that before we built our mountain house. It's good for both you and your young person to see that "special one" in a different situation, one in which he or she must depend upon his or her own resources for a good time. Too often, a couple is "entertained" for their entire courtship, either by dinners in fancy restaurants or else by movies,

TV, planned activities at church, miniature golf, bowling, and all the other trappings that are provided by society to amuse us. Marriage isn't a series of expensive evenings out, but more often a night-after-night staying at home together, particularly after the babies come. If the couple can't fellowship together happily without outside resources, there is trouble ahead.

The Bible talks a lot about being hospitable, and I don't believe this means only to other adults. Our homes should be open to our children's friends and dates, too. So often as our teenagers were in high school and college, other mothers would say to me, "I don't know how you can stand all those kids around—I just wouldn't permit it at my house!" It was hard for them to believe that we really enjoyed them, but we loved every minute of it. They were more interesting than a lot of adults we met, and much more open and loving. Looking back on it now, I wouldn't trade any of the time we spent with those young people for coffee klatches with neighbors, shopping trips, or sophisticated luncheons with my lady friends. The needs of those kids whose mothers wouldn't permit them to be at their own homes with their friends were more important than any selfish interests I might have had.

If you are nervous around teenagers or just plain can't stand to have them around, ask God to give you a special burden and love for them. There aren't nearly enough people who care about them, and perhaps this is why they spend so much time seeking and finding the wrong things in life. They want love, understanding, and acceptance, as we all do, and if they get it at your home you will benefit in the long run by being able to know intimately those who are your children's friends and dates. Remember, dates often turn into mates, so if you treat them all in a loving way, you won't have a problem if they become part of your family.

2

A Diamond Is Forever

Courtship and Engagement

"Mom, isn't she wonderful?" our son, Gary, said after an evening that he and his girlfriend, Dorene, had spent with us. I knew in my heart at that moment that this was "the one." Things moved rapidly after that—long talks about marriage and asking her father's permission, shopping for a ring, setting a wedding date. It was all so exciting and we were so pleased with his choice.

Number one for the groom's parents in the etiquette book is to invite the bride's parents to meet them, if they haven't before. When our oldest son, Jeff, was married, I knew his fiancee's mother from attending high-school football games. Jeff was a star halfback and Pattie was a song girl. When they became engaged we invited Pattie's parents over so our husbands could meet each other. They had similar jobs, loved golf and sports, and liked to play games, so they had no problem establishing a rapport.

We had not met our daughter's in-laws when she became engaged, as they lived in another town close by. Nancy told us they were rather shy people, so we took the initiative and invited them for a weekend at our cabin. They too had common interests with us—Jim's dad loved sports, is a handyman around the house (as my husband is), and plays golf. They enjoy camping, too, and we have taken many camping trips with both families.

When Gary became engaged, and as we made arrangements to have Dorene's parents over for dinner, we began to ask him questions about their interest. "Does her dad play golf?" I asked Gary. "No," he said, "But he likes to ski." George and I hadn't skied since college because of a knee injury he had. "Well, how about fishing—does he like to fish?" "He water skis," Gary replied. We love to swim, but neither of us water skis. "Oh, well, is he interested in sports? He probably likes football." "I don't believe so," he answered. "He didn't watch the Super Bowl."

When I questioned Gary further as to Dorene's dad's interests, I found that he is a commercial photographer and therefore very interested in that field. My husband is probably the world's most unwilling picture-taker. All of our albums are filled with pictures of him and our children, while I appear maybe once or twice a year. I take all the pictures and enjoy keeping up the albums. Her parents have a boat and enjoy that, while we have a cabin. They love to take motorcycle trips and to camp, while we have a tent-trailer.

Needless to say, after this conversation with Gary, I was on pins and needles about having Dorene's parents to dinner. I kept asking my husband what we would talk about, and he kept telling me not to worry about it. "What if they don't like us?" I said. "Lou, trust the Lord!" he would answer. At last the fateful night came, and this sweet, friendly couple appeared at our door—middle-aged, just like us. They were down-to-earth, easy to talk with, and interested in everything. We had a delightful evening and talked so much that, before we realized it, it was almost midnight on a Tuesday night. All my worrying was simply a lack of faith, and later I found out from Dorene that her parents were just as nervous about meeting us as we were about meeting them!

Being warm and friendly to our prospective in-law's family is important, but even more urgent is our initial reaction to that young person. It should be one of open, friendly, loving kindness. If the young man or woman is made to feel comfortable and welcome in our home, the couple will spend time there and we can get to know them better. If the atmosphere is formal and polite, chances are that he or she will become a fixture at the home of the other in-laws or, if he is not living with parents, at his apartment. In this case, when he marries we really won't have gotten to know his mate very well, and it will make a close relationship more difficult to establish.

One suggestion based on our experience is to try to set up a one-night-a-week dinner with the couple. Be sure to be flexible on this, and don't be upset if they can't make it part of the time. Remember that they have obligations and unexpected events which come up, just as you do. Mealtimes should be casual. When our son-in-law or daughters-in-law-to-be came to dinner, we ate at our round kitchen table rather than in the dining room. I used place mats instead of table cloths (this is our nightly pattern), and if we were having leftovers, I didn't change plans because they were there. I wanted them to feel comfortable, and it isn't as easy when we set a "company" table.

Sometimes my husband and I took them out to dinner at the neighborhood steak house or pizza parlor. Other times we splurged and took them to a nice restaurant. If I had had an especially busy day, we would even send out for a fast-food dinner. Other times we had additional friends over and had a more formal dinner in the dining room. We made sure the prospective in-law saw us in all kinds of situations to get to know us as we really are.

It is important to realize that there may be things about your son- or daughter-in-law-to-be that you wish would change. And take heart—they probably will change. When our daughter began going with her husband, the only reservation I had was the fact that she had more education than he, and that she had always, from a small girl, wanted to marry a minister. He was a partner in a construction firm, and I hoped that she would never be sorry that she didn't marry someone in the full-time ministry. He was such a wonderful young man that we didn't have any other objections, and we were excited about the wedding.

About a year after they were married, his firm was sold to another company and he made a momentous decision—you guessed it—to study for the ministry. The one small objection I would have had to the marriage was wiped out as he graduated from an excellent Bible college and began his work as a youth pastor. He is a fine husband and father and has made our daughter happier than we had even hoped. I believe *any* mother-in-law could get along well with him, and my husband I have grown to love him more and more over the years. I don't mean to single out my son-in-law—I love my daughters-in-law just as much!

Even if the prospective mate of your child has qualities that are, as far as you can see, serious drawbacks, give the situation to the Lord, love that person, and trust that He will work it out for the best. Part of what you see as a drawback may be something that God is already working on to change, and part of it may be your own reservation toward him or her. Maybe you are not as warm and loving toward him as you could be. Perhaps you are overly sensitive, and if he has a very outgoing temperament, he may hurt your feelings without intending to or without even being aware of it.

Some gregarious people tend to speak before they think, and often it comes out wrong, particularly if they are nervous. (Just ask me—I've done it often enough.) Some people enter a room mouth-first, and spend their whole time filling the silences in conversation. Be understanding and try to put them at ease so that they won't feel they have to talk all the time. If your own relationship with the Lord is in tune and you are walking closely with Him, you will find it much easier to love this new family member. You will be flexible in accepting his or her weak points, recognizing that he or she must accept yours, too.

I believe the saddest answer to any of the questions on the mother-in-law survey was number 48: "Do you know for sure that your mother-in-law really loves you?" Half of those who answered said no. Small wonder that mothers-in-law have a bad reputation as a group! The Bible says that Christians should be known by their love for one another. If we cannot find love in our hearts to express to the one whom our own child has been given by God, how can we love *anyone* outside our family?

The Bible says in 1 John that if we don't love each other, we don't even love God. Maybe you have trouble being demonstrative, so that those you love are not sure that you love them. In that case, pray that God will give you the desire to change and to show your love in an outward, obvious way to your family. John 8:32 says, "You shall know the truth, and the truth shall make you free." The truth is that God is love and He desires above all else that we love each other. The freedom that comes from this truth will allow you to express that love openly, and your love will be returned by that new member of the family and will give you a closeness you never dreamed possible.

My husband and I both hug our son-in-law and daughters-in-law each time they come to our home, and kiss them if they've been away for a long time. We do the same to our own children, of course, and always have. We began doing this with the in-law kids as soon as they become engaged. We even hug their parents when they come for a visit, and at a family potluck or holiday there are "holy hugs" for everyone. Don't be afraid to show affection and verbalize your love for these new family members. If they ever fill out a mother-in-law survey, make sure their answer to question 48 is a positive *yes!*

An important facet in building a love relationship with your son- or daughter-in-law is letting your own child go—untying the apron strings, as the saying goes. Many mothers find this an extremely difficult thing to do. Some think they have let go while they really have not, and others do not just *untie* them but sever them completely. A balance in your relationship is necessary if it is to glorify God. We must be available when they need us but not interfering. Think of God's way of dealing with us: He is always available to us when we call on Him, but He does not interfere in our lives. We should be helpful but not interfering, and there is a fine line between the two.

Many mothers have told me that they feel a certain jealousy toward this new person who is the center of their child's life. This is a trap of Satan, who wants us to be selfish and self-centered because it ruins our witness as Christian mothers-in-law. There is plenty of room in our son's or daughter's heart for us as well as the one he or she marries. Think of yourself—you still loved your mother when you married your husband, but it was a different type of love.

Our children weren't given to us as possessions

to keep forever; they were loaned to us by God to train up in His way and to honor Him with their lives. They cannot do this if we stifle their spirits by keeping them tied to us rather than letting them pursue their own lives the way God leads. I have always looked forward to the time when all my children would be happily married with families of their own. That has been my goal for them in life, second only to the wish that they would love the Lord and put Him first. Praise the Lord! He has allowed me to see the fulfillment of that goal, although the two newest-wed couples do not have children as yet.

If you are not sure you have a balanced relationship with your child and his fiancee, ask yourself the following questions and answer them as honestly as you can.

1. Do you get hurt feelings when you are not included in the plans of the engaged couple or when they fail to spend time you you?

2. Are you still treating your engaged child as you did when he or she was in school, checking on his whereabouts and expecting him to be home at certain hours?

3. Are you making decisions for the engaged couple that they should be making alone (such as helping to choose their home, furnishings, location, job, size of family, etc.)?

4. Are you playing the martyr by refusing to give them advice when they seek your counsel or by being negative about their plans?

5. Are you unwilling to let them learn by their own mistakes? A good idea is to offer a suggestion

once if you see that they are about to make an unwise decision; then pray about it and leave it up to the Lord.

If you answered any of these questions in the affirmative, that is the area that could be a potential problem. Ask God to guide you in your actions toward the engaged couple and to give you His wisdom in being the kind of mother-in-law that He would have you be.

3

Here Comes The Bride

The Wedding

As the big day draws nearer, there is more strain on human relationships. If your daughter is the bride, there may be tears of frustration over small details. If your son is the bridegroom, expect him to be moody at times, forgetful at other times, or defensive when you offer suggestions. Marriage is a big step, and the responsibility of it all may be worrying him. Since the problems of being a bride or groom are unique to each situation, we will approach them separately.

The mother of the bride has by far the biggest responsibility in the wedding. Since the bride's parents sponsor the wedding and reception, the bride chooses the attire worn, the type of ceremony, and whether it will be a simple cake-and-punch fellowship time afterward or a lavish dinner with all the trimmings. All of this should be subject to the groom's approval, of course, but it has been our experience that most bridegrooms defer to the bride's wishes as far as the wedding ceremony.

In all fairness, whatever you are willing to do for daughter number 1 should also be offered when subsequent daughters are married, unless circumstances change drastically, such as ill health or loss of financial security. We had only one daughter, so we were able to give her a large wedding and reception. We have been careful, however, to make certain that we were equally generous with each child regarding wedding gifts, helping the boys pay for a nice honeymoon and being ready to make a loan to help with a down payment on a home or business venture, if it was needed. We have known parents who have given an extravagant wedding to their first child, only to have a second one unexpectedly decide to get married within the same year, causing a real hardship financially or making it necessary to skimp on the second wedding. Be sure to take this into consideration when you are planning.

One important aspect of preparing for a wedding is making sure that the groom's parents are included in the plans. Usually the mother and daughter shop for the wedding dress, but when it has been chosen, the groom's mother (and sisters, if he has them) should be taken to see it. The groom's mother should be informed as to the size and type of wedding and reception and how many people she may include in her guest list.

This last item has been one which has been the source of dissension in many of my friends' children's weddings. I have come to the conclusion that it is better to have a cake-and-punch reception and include all the friends of both sides of the family than to have an expensive buffet for just a limited number of people. Cutting people off a guest list is a terribly frustrating experience, and I have listened to the complaints of many mothers-of-grooms as they attempt to pick and choose who will be able to attend and who will not. I am so thankful that we were able to invite all of our family, far and near, as well as all our friends and neighbors—those with whom my husband worked, casual friends at church with whom we've served with over the years, and our children's classmates. This way we didn't have to worry about hurting anyone's feelings.

One lady I know was limited to 30 invitations, even though the church was large, because the mother of the bride wanted a small reception. Her husband was one of seven children, and by the time they mailed an invitation to each of the relatives, they were unable to ask more than three or four couples who were very close friends; they had to eliminate all their neighbors and those with whom they both worked. It really spoiled the wedding for the couple because they had attended so many weddings of people whom they were unable to include in their own wedding. This can mean a poor start in the relationship between the bride's family and the groom's relatives, and it would be wiser to have a less costly reception and be on good terms with the other in-laws.

The groom's family usually puts on the rehearsal dinner, and his mother will need your list of guests. These are normally the bridal party, visiting relatives from out of town, and dates or mates of the bridal attendants. It can be held at home, at a restaurant, or at your church hall. A catered affair, even if it is just the bridal committee from church, is much easier and more enjoyable for the mother of the groom than having to prepare the food herself. If finances do not permit this, be sure to ask friends and relatives to help.

It would be courteous, if you are the bride's mother, to ask the mother of the groom if she has any suggestions as to photographer, caterer, florist, etc. (if she has put on a wedding for her daughter.) She is probably as anxious to have good family relations as you are, and will do her best to be helpful. This is not a book of wedding etiquette, so we will not go into that. I would suggest the booklet *Checklist for a Perfect Wedding,* available at department stores. Weddings have become much less formal, and there is more freedom today in doing what the bride and groom prefer than used to be the custom.

Talk to friends and to your wedding consultant at church, and then give the whole thing over to the Lord and pray for His blessing. Be flexible and don't have set ideas that you don't want to change. It is more important that the young people be satisfied with their wedding than to have your own way. Your relationship with the other mother at this point will depend upon how you get along in the planning stage. When Pattie and her mother and I were ordering the flowers for her and Jeff's wedding, the florist commented on how well we got along and what fun we were having together. We were joking and laughing and both deferring to the other's wishes in every way possible, and the florist said that so many families come in and argue and become angry with each other while choosing flowers and decorations.

One suggestion that I feel is very important is to choose the best photographer available. Even if you feel you have to limit your spending, that is the last place to cut down. The pictures are what you have after the wedding is over, and if they are a disappointment, you will be very sorry. I still thumb through my children's wedding albums almost weekly, reliving those precious moments. Our grandchildren like nothing better than to look at mommy and daddy getting married, and with the great expense of weddings it is nice to have something to remember them by.

A few suggestions gained from my experience with four weddings are as follows:

1. Do have pictorial invitations. We have received so many of these in the past few years, and we enjoy them so much. There are many different styles, and they are especially nice for those relatives and friends who live out of town and cannot be at the wedding.

2. Try wholesale-distributing companies for paper plates, cups, punch mix, plastic forks, and spoons. They will often sell them to the public at wholesale costs.

3. Instead of the traditional favors with almonds inside, try little scrolls with a printed note

inside from the bride and groom, thanking the guests for attending.

4. Begin serving as soon as people enter the reception hall, if you are having a buffet or finger food. It gives them something to do while the photographs are being taken. If you are serving cake and punch, offer the drinks as people are waiting for the cake to be cut.

5. Take as many pictures before the wedding as possible, so that the reception won't be delayed.

6. If you are serving a buffet at the reception, prepare a small cooler chest for the bride and groom to take with them on their honeymoon. Our newlyweds all appreciated this because they did not have to go out to dinner that evening but could relax at their hotel or resort after the big day.

7. Make it a point to enjoy the preparations and the wedding. It's a once-in-a-lifetime affair, and I have yet to see a wedding that wasn't a success, or where anything serious went wrong. Be as organized as you can, pray for the Lord to remind you of everything important, and have fun!

4

Getting To Know You

The First Year

Life is full of adjustments—from the time we decide to take away the pacifer on a permanent basis to that goodbye wave as our offspring drives off in a gaily decorated honeymoon car. We can remember the first night out of the crib and into the "big bed." The first day at school is always traumatic for mom, as is the first night of "sleeping over" at a friend's house. When our daughter, Nancy, was five years old, she begged to be allowed to sleep next door at her girlfriend's home. At 2:00 AM the doorbell rang and there was Laurie's father, handing us a blanket-wrapped, tear-streaked little girl who got lonesome when she woke up in the middle of the night. The next week the whole process was reversed as my husband carried our neighbor girl back to *her* house around midnight!

Then there was the first time away from home

at church camp. (Would those delapidated buses make it up that long hill?) The first day of high school sneaks up on us, and that scary experience, the first date. The senior prom, graduation, college, jobs—all were adjustments, or what is more commonly called "phases." But at least we as parents still have some semblance of control during these times. After the wedding, the adjustment is often difficult and may hurt a little. Happy as we are that they've finally found their life partner, we are in a whole new relationship with the child to whom we've given birth and whom we've raised to adulthood.

Our actions (and reactions) during this first year of marriage will set the tone of our relationship for the remainder of our lives. If we are demanding, pouting, and reserved, or else loving, understanding, and open, we are sowing these seeds to be treated in like manner. Galatians 6:7 says that whatever a man sows, this he will also reap. That is a biblical concept which is true, and that's why God tells us to do unto others as we would have them do to us. We can drive that delightful newlywed couple away with authoritative attitudes, by being demanding, by having hurt feelings because they don't pay us enough attention, or by requiring too much of them. They need time alone to get to know each other in a way that will make easy their communication as a couple.

All my life I've heard people say, "You never know someone until you're married to them!" And it's true. My daughters-in-law have discovered things about my sons of which I was completely oblivious. I am very close to my daughter, but I'm sure my son-in-law could tell me much about her that I don't know. Of all the people in the world, there is nobody I know like I know my husband.

Day-to-day living in a love relationship with another person in the framework of marriage produces knowledge about that mate that nothing else will reveal. Only the security of marriage can make us free to be ourselves and to bare our innermost feelings to another person. Our own children will not share those things with us which may embarrass them because they are afraid of ridicule or a lecture. A young couple needs this "letting-down" time as they begin to let their real selves surface and share their deep needs, goals, and dreams with each other.

An important lesson for us to learn at this time is to keep advice to a minimum. If we only give it when it is asked for, that's pretty safe. And the manner in which we give it is as important as the advice itself. Don't deliver it as an oratory or an ultimatum with the implication that if they choose not to follow it, they are little more than idiots. Give them a choice, if possible, of two or more alternatives. Explore the possible results of the various courses, and be objective. Help them to see the wisdom of a decision along with the impression that it has been their own choice. And if they decide upon *their* way and not yours, don't say "I told you so" if it backfires. They will learn from their mistakes, just as we all have. God may be teaching them a lesson that can only be learned through failure.

We have seen in-laws put pressure on a young couple to the point where they have completely alienated them and even damaged the relationship between the newlyweds. One overzealous mother-in-law insisted upon doing their house-hunting for them. Since she was helping them with the down payment, they felt obligated to let her have her way. This well-meaning lady toured the city with a real-estate agent, chose the house she thought was best for them, took them to see it, and pressured them to buy it. It was a nice home and her choice wasn't bad, but it was *her* choice, not theirs. Her son was happy with the house, but her daughter-in-law confided to friends that she hated it. I don't believe she really hated the house, but the fact that she had no choice in the matter. A woman's home is her castle, and it should be a castle of her own choosing.

When my husband graduated from college, we moved to Seattle and bought a partially completed house in a new area south of the city. We had very little money, and the home we bought has been a source of amusement to us through the years. My husband was raised in a small town where lots were large, so we bought a small house on about 1 ½ aces. When we brought our relatives to see our new investment, it must have been a terrible shock. The fact that no one laughed or made disparaging remarks is a credit to their sensitivity. The floor plan was terribly inconvenient. The bathroom was next to the kitchen table, and it was necessary to walk through the living room to get to the dining room. The flooring was plywood and the walls were fiberboard, which we covered with several inches of Spackle. There was no closet in one bedroom, so we made that into a nursery for our firstborn, who arrived 11 months after we moved in.

Realizing the drawbacks of this house without anyone telling us about them, we sold it shortly after our son was born and bought a "real" house. We learned a lot through the error we made in the purchase of that first house, and we were much more discriminating in our house-hunting from that time on. And we learned another important fact: it is *wise* to ask for advice! Allow your children this same freedom of choice so that they can learn from their own mistakes.

During the first year we have made it a policy to visit our married children only when invited. After the first year we sometimes call and ask if they are going to be home and if a visit will be convenient. I am not too fond of surprise guests, as they usually manage to catch me and my home at our worst. I've had unexpected company when I was in the shower, coloring my hair, cleaning my oven, going out the door to a previous appointment, entertaining other guests, rearranging furniture, or lying sick in bed. It's embarrassing to be seen with our hair full of suds, and I appreciate a call letting me know that a friend is in the area and would like to come by for a visit. I treat my children with this same courtesy. We invite our married children to dinner every couple of weeks, and when they ask us we babysit for them (if we are available). Otherwise we let them make the decision as to when they wish to get together with us.

This first year of marriage will set a pattern for future life relationships with our married children. It's much easier to get off on the right foot than it is to repair the damage if we set some bad patterns. When our daughter was married, we didn't really see her and her husband very often that first year. However, now that they've been married five years and there are two grandchildren, we find that we see them very often—at least once a week. When we allow our newly married young ones to break the ties and establish their own lives, they do not feel threatened by us and are free to begin to spend more time with us and become good friends on an equal basis. We are flattered when they invite us to spend their vacations with them, and we enjoy holidays and occasional weekends and dinners with them.

I believe that if we push ourselves into our children's lives after they marry, they will back off from us and feel pressured when they spend time with us. We would much rather have them get together with us because they *choose* to than because they feel obligated to. Untie those apron strings and you will find that you have a whole new set of best friends—your married kids!

5

All In The Family

The Problem Mother-in-Law

Hopefully, this book will prevent many a crisis in your life when your children marry. But what of those parents who have married children and already have problems in the relationship with them? Recently, when I was in the Midwest doing a Fulfilled Woman Seminar, a lady came up to me and said, "I wish you'd hurry up and finish that mother-in-law book! I've been a mother-in-law three weeks and I've already blown it!" Even if this is your case, all is not lost. Proverbs 21:1 says, "The king's heart is in the hand of the Lord, as are the watercourses; He turns it whichever way He will." In other words, God is in control, and He can change people's minds, repair damaged relationships, and turn friction into fellowship.

There are three types of problem in-laws: your own mother-in-law, your son-in-law or daughter-in-law, and your child's mother-in-law. We will deal with each of these separately, because the problems are usually different with each one. There are probably in-law problems of which I have never heard, and we will be taking only the most common ones into consideration here. Whenever there is a family problem, I believe the best way to solve it is through the principles taught in God's Word, and that is where we are going to go to find the solutions to them. If you are in the Word daily, God will help you to find your own solutions, but if you are a new Christian or unfamiliar with biblical principles, we will learn to apply them together.

Let's look at the different types of mothers-in-law and try to place yours into the category that most nearly fits her. She isn't going to be a carbon copy of these ladies, but you will find her characteristics fitting one of them more closely than the others.

Domineering Dora

This is the mother-in-law whose own home is out of order. She wears the pants in the family while her husband is "Henpecked Harry," who long ago gave up opposing her openly. She makes the decisions about what they purchase, where they go on vacation, their social life, and even what car they drive. She handles the finances, chooses his clothes, and tells him what to eat and what time to go to bed. He finds it easier to go along with her than to discuss it, as it always ends up in an argument, which she wins because she can yell the loudest and hold out the longest.

This mother-in-law begins coming on strong as soon as you are engaged. If she is the mother of the bride, she completely takes over the wedding plans, allowing her daughter little voice in the decisions and the groom's family none whatsoever. She may plan the entire wedding without even asking the daughter's opinion or desires. If the bride expresses a wish for anything not in accordance with her mother's ideas, she is quickly set straight and reminded about who is paying for the wedding.

We went to a wedding once where the mother walked down the aisle with the bride, and it was difficult to see the bride at all with her mother on one side, her father on the other, and her squashed in-between. If this bossy lady is the mother of the groom, she immediately begins calling the bride and her mother to offer "helpful suggestions."

Domineering Dora will try to choose where and how the young couple will live and what type of dishes, china, and furniture they should have. She may even attempt to pick their friends and plan their social activities. She will often try to influence what church they should attend, especially if it's different from hers. If she is not a Christian, she will discourage them from becoming "religious fanatics." When the children begin arriving, the couple will often wonder whether they are "theirs" or "hers." Dora is the type of mother-in-law who can actually break up a marriage if she has a weak child and has him or her completely under her thumb. I know personally of two cases where this has happened. So what is the answer to handling this kind of mother-in-law?

If it is your wife's mother, your position may be somewhat easier. You are the head of the family, and you must assert yourself (Ephesians 5:22-33). If your wife is dominated by her mother, it will be easier for her to transfer her submissive attitude to you. Dora's "Mack truck" traits are a result of her husband's lack of leadership in the family. She secretly resents being boss, and it has given her a deep-seated hostility and lack of respect for men in general. When she sees that she cannot run your life for you and that you will not give in when you sincerely believe you are right on an important issue, her respect for you will grow, especially if you are loving and flattering to her.

Being assertive does not mean being cross or cutting her down. It means taking a firm stand but doing it in a charming way. Joke with her, be affectionate, and let her know that although her idea is a good one, you feel that in this instance you want to please your wife, or that it is best for the welfare of your family in the long run. Intimate that you were sure she would be understanding, and tell her how much you appreciate her support. You can handle the situation diplomatically, so that when you are through explaining it to her, she will think that the change of plans was her own idea. Develop an attitude of "fellow conspirators" with her, and she will love you for it. Ask her opinion on unimportant matters and then follow her advice. She will think she is playing an indispensable role, and when you do not follow her advice, it won't be so hard to take.

Tenacious Tillie

This is the woman with the "My Son" syndrome; absolutely NO ONE is good enough for him. You could be a combination of Ruth, Esther, and the Virgin Mary and she would still turn thumbs down on you. She is the most difficult mother-in-law of all, being critical of you and overly possessive of her son. She is the type whose son was "all boy" while he was growing up, in her eyes. Others would be more inclined to describe him as "all brat."

He grew into a pretty nice guy in spite of it, and you married him. However, to dear old mom he is still her "baby" and always will be. This mother-in-law is usually less than happily married herself and has made her children the center of her life instead of Jesus Christ. She has few outside interests and is constantly on the lookout for things she can criticize in you—your cooking, housekeeping, appearance, personality, spending habits, and treatment of her son. If this is your situation, here are some pointers which may help you.

1. Recognize that it is *her* problem, not yours, and give it to God. First Peter 5:7 says, "Cast all your anxiety upon Him, for He cares for you." It is almost impossible to please your mother-in-law, so don't worry about it. Make sure your own relationship is right with God and right with your husband; do the best you can as a homemaker, and don't take it personally when she criticizes you. Just remember that whoever had married her son would receive the same treatment as you.

2. Don't try to defend yourself to her, argue

with her, or become angry. That's a tall order, but you can do all things through Christ, who strengthens you (Philippians 4:13). Remember that God vindicates His children. If her criticism is valid, try to improve. Ask her for pointers and how *she* does things. God gave you that mother-in-law to help mold you into the kind of woman he wants you to be. Praise Him for it and ask Him what He wants you to learn from the situation.

3. Pray for God's love for your mother-in-law. Ask Him to love her through you. Pray for her every day, and you will begin to understand her problems and insecurities, and it will help your feelings toward her. Don't force your husband to take sides—it will put a strain on your marriage. Ask God to help you see her through His eyes, and you will be surprised at what you see.

4. Don't be afraid to admit you are wrong.

    a. A bad relationship is seldom only one person's fault.

    b. You may have responded wrongly to her and hurt her feelings.

    c. Consider her criticisms as from the Lord, or, if you know that are unwarranted, overlook them.

    d. Pray for her faithfully; ask God to show you her needs.

    e. Make it a point to visit her regularly, if possible.

    f. If she is a hypochondriac, try to be sympathetic; she may need more attention.

    g. Pray with her, if possible.

h   Never criticize her to others.
i.   Don't complain about her to your husband; it puts him on the defensive and forces him to take your side against her.
j.   Do thoughtful things for her; an inexpensive gift, a book, a card, or some cologne will brighten her day.
k.   Let her see her grandchildren often.

5. Pray for areas where God shows you she needs help, and ask Him to show you creative alternatives to rectify the situation. If she is not a Christian, pray for her salvation. If she is a Christian, try to attend a Bible study together.

Martha Martyr

This is the type of mother-in-law who, as Erma Bombeck says, takes her tape recorder to the delivery room and plays it back at her children's weddings. She is the ''worked her fingers to the bone for you'' mother, and she is ''in complete misery.'' She also sees to it that everyone else is, too. She is definitely a hypochondriac—the doctors can never find anything seriously wrong with her, but she runs from one doctor to another, insisting that they are missing whatever it is she believes she has. She is extremely hard to please: if you visit her, you don't stay long enough or stay too long and the children make her nervous. If you don't see her often, you're an ungrateful person and she will pout all the time you are there when you do come. If you call her, she will answer the telephone with her ''sickly'' voice, but as you visit, she will forget and speak normally. If she has a husband, she dumps part of her load of cares on him, but if she's a widow or divorced, you get the *whole* thing!

Her feelings are easily hurt, and she carries a grudge, so you are seldom in her good graces. Gifts please her, but only if they are expensive and she can boast about them to her friends. She seldom is active in any organization because she manages to alienate everyone who gets involved with her either through her constant complaining, imaginary ill-nesses, or hurt feelings. This poor lady has real problems in self-acceptance and selfishness. Her whole world is centered around herself, and it is impossible for her to be sensitive to anyone else. She believes that everyone is out to take advantage of her and is usually quite miserly with her money. Denying herself pleasures helps her martyr complex, and she "enjoys" complaining.

This most impossible mother-in-law requires much prayer. Pray that God will give you His love for her and show her to you through His eyes. She has very deep personality problems and probably needs professional counseling. If she lives close to you, taking her to church and attempting to get her involved there will help. If she does not, you are probably fortunate. If she does live close by and is antagonistic toward Christianity, the prob-lem is compounded. Prayer is the only answer because only God knows how to solve the prob-lem. Treading softly and carefully will be difficult but it is the only way you can stay friends. Just make sure your own relationship with the Lord is

right, so that it will be easier to accept the burden
of her personality.

Sarah Subtle

This gentle-voiced mother-in-law will push
you—as far as you will go to do her bidding. You
will not, however, be aware of it until you realize
that you have rearranged your entire lifestyle to suit
her. One unsuspecting bride-to-be altered her complete wedding plans before she awoke to the fact that
the ceremony, attire, and reception were what her
mother-in-law wanted and **not** what she herself
desired. One ''subtle'' suggestion after another had
been injected until Sarah had ruined the wedding for
her prospective daughter-in-law.

Sarah makes a scene when she doesn't get her
own way, but it is a quiet one. She gets up in the
middle of a conversation, sniffling just audibly
enough for others to hear, and goes to her room,
where she remains until someone comes to get her.
She doesn't *seem* demanding; she merely offers
suggestions which she feels are perfectly
reasonable and sheds a few tears (quietly, of
course) until someone capitulates to her and things
go as she planned.

A couple who lived in Los Angeles told of the
problem of their in-laws' annual visit to Southern
California each year. The young couple would re-
quest that the in-laws plan to arrive at the Los
Angeles airport during the morning, early after-
noon, or late evening so they would not be caught
in the hectic rush-hour traffic. They explained that
during the busy time the drive to the airport could

take up to two hours each way. Each year the letter would come announcing their arrival on the 5:15 P.M. flight.

Finally, after years of ignored requests, the couple decided to take a firm stand. When notification of the 5:15 P.M. arrival came, they called the following message: "Since you have chosen to come during the rush hour, we're sure you will not mind catching the bus from the airport. It will take you directly to a hotel near our house, and we will pick you up there." The in-laws, realizing that the couple was serious, immediately changed their reservations to a plane convenient to their children's schedule.

This seems to be the best procedure to take with a mother-in-law such as Sarah Subtle. A forthright approach is necessary to bring her innuendos and veiled suggestions out into the open and pin her down to a definite plan. If she is allowed to subtly manipulate behind the scenes, it will go on forever, with her always getting her own way and you coming out on the short end. Complete, loving honesty is always the best approach. If she insists on continuing with her own plans in spite of you, then let her take the bus or its equivalent.

Isabel Ignore

Isabel is the type of mother-in-law who buries her head in the sand and pretends that her son (or daughter) isn't married. It's almost as if by ignoring the in-law he will suddenly disappear and she will again have her own chick back in the nest. She's the in-law who has the mother's ring made up with her own children and grandchildren birthstones while leaving out their husband or wife. She requests a family picture with "just Sonny and the children, please—the blood relatives you know." Vacation visits are extended to her daughter and grandchildren at a time when she is sure her son-in-law won't be able to make it.

At Christmas, Isabel may lavish expensive gifts on her grandchildren and son or daughter, but give only a token present to the in-law. She conveniently "forgets" any birthday of anyone she considers "outside" the family. And believe me, the in-law is made to feel that he or she is an outsider. She often plans conflicting family get-togethers, with no thought at all for the other in-laws. When she visits, she may even cook special little meals for her son, to be enjoyed by no one else. If there are no children on the scene as yet, Isabel will often invite her son or daughter to stop by "alone" so they can have a "private" visit. (There is certainly nothing wrong with an occasional get-together between a mother and her married son or daughter unless it becomes a habitual thing or a definite exclusion of the husband or wife.)

Isabel Ignore may even have favorites among her in-law kids, excluding only one or two of them. My grandmother definitely preferred my aunt's husband to her other two in-laws, and she would visit them, invite them to dinner, and give them financial aid and other gifts while ignoring her daughter-in-law and other son-in-law. My mother and uncle got to the point of visiting her without their mates because she so obviously disregarded them while they were in her home. She would direct all her conversation to someone else. Poor Grandma missed a lot of good fellowship!

Handling this unrealistic mother-in-law requires a very tenacious spirit. Pray for God to show you ways to relate to her and to prove that you do exist. A good plan would be to get together with her when your mate is not present. Perhaps she is afraid of you, and by refusing to admit your presence in her life she is doing what she can to alleviate her fears. Fear of the unknown disappears when it becomes familiar. If you can open up to her, ask her advice or her expertise in some area where she excels (like cooking, sewing, crafts, knitting, etc.). This may be just what is needed to develop a good relationship with her. As she becomes more intimately acquainted with you, she will lose her feeling of whatever she fears will happen as a result of your being part of the family. Possibly she thinks you will usurp her authority or challenge her position. We all have certain functions in the life of our family, and when she realizes that hers and yours are entirely different, perhaps she will not feel threatened.

If she is a Christian, asking her to pray with you would be very helpful in developing your relationship. If she is not a Christian, she is probably not going to change. Older people rarely do without the help of Christ, and you as a Christian are going to have to take the initiative in giving of yourself. You will need to be loving, understanding, and self-sacrificing. First Peter 4:14 says, "If you are insulted because of the name of

Christ, you are blessed, for the Spirit of glory and of God rests on you'' (NIV). This is a promise from God, and perhaps your willingness to bear the pain of this relationship will result in your mother-in-law's conversion. It is not what we believe that leads others to the Savior, but the way we behave.

Paula Polite

Unfortunately, Paula is a very common type of mother-in-law. She probably outrates the others two to one, according to conversations I've had with those who have mother-in-law problems. She is always reserved, cool, and distant, and she treats her in-law kids like uninvited guests. She is much less warm to them than to casual friends or acquaintances, to whom she puts her best foot forward in order to make a good impression.

One young woman said, ''My mother-in-law always treats me as a guest, when what I want to be is a member of the family!'' She was never allowed to help with meals or holiday preparations but was asked to stay in the living room. She was even excluded from family discussions of a serious nature, and information that was shared with close friends was kept from her. If a pregnancy or marriage was imminent in the family, she would learn the news from a mutual friend. (Her husband often knew, but, as with most men, those things are not uppermost in his mind and he would forget to tell her.) She was made to feel that she was less a part of the family than the most casual acquaintance. Conversation when she was present was always kept in a very general vein, and nothing of consequence was ever discussed in front of her.

Paula Polite would be shocked if anyone suggested that she was less than a perfect mother-in-law. Her problem generally stems from self-centeredness combined with a naturally reserved personality. She is not thinking of the welfare of her daugher-in-law or son-in-law, but only of her resentment at having an extra member of the family whom she did not personally select. Maybe she has valid objections to the new in-law. Perhaps before the marriage there was a strained relationship which Paula cannot overlook. Often if a couple has had a live-together arrangement before marriage, their mothers find it hard to forgive them and tend to falsely blame the in-law child for leading her own child into such a relationship. They do not realize that it takes two people to arrive at such a decision. She may be allowing the bitterness which was present toward them before their marriage influence her feelings toward them afterward. This will only bring unhappiness to all concerned and God is very vocal to us regarding an unforgiving heart.

If this was your case, in which your mother-in-law was hurt by something which occurred before your marriage, try to understand her feelings. Put yourself in her shoes and attempt to discern what your reactions would be if your children were to hurt you in a similar way. Possibly you should go to her and apologize for your actions and ask her forgiveness.

I have known young people who lived unacceptable lifestyles before they became Christians but who have completely changed their attitudes and have been forgiven by God. However, they have neglected to ask forgiveness of those who love them who were so hurt by their former actions. Persons with melancholy temperaments have a hard time getting over their hurts, and tend to nurse grudges and dwell on the past. If you believe that you have hurt your mother-in-law at any time, be sure to make amends with her.

If, however, you honestly do not know why she won't accept you, discuss this with your husband in a calm, loving way. Possibly she treats all her in-law children the same way. If this is so, you could make a group effort to loosen her up. If it is just you who is on the receiving end of her coolness, perhaps your husband can find out what the problem is, and together you can rectify the situation with her. Pray for wisdom and for God to change her heart, using Proverbs 21:1 as a promise to claim, and ask Him to help her be more open to having a loving relationship with you.

Rita Ruckus

If I hadn't known so many mothers-in-law like Rita, I would not believe she was a real character. Rita is not a Christian, and her favorite hobby is getting a rousing disagreement going in her family. She is then in her element as the center of attention as she plies first one member and then another with shaded truths and exaggerated stories of what one said about the other, or about her. She often mentions her will and how each one is trying to outdo the other in getting her to leave them her money or property. Once she gets dissension stirred up, she keeps the "mix" button on so that it will keep going.

If there is a pacifist in the family, Rita will probably refuse to speak to that one at all, for fear that the problem will become settled and the ruckus will end. Rita delights in repeating gossip and will twist the most innocent remark in order to use it on one member of the family against another. There will be just enough truth in it to make it believable but enough untruth to make it deadly.

Rita is a very selfish, bitter woman who is only interested in being the pretended referee in the family fights. She will purposely indulge one member of the family with gifts or financial help while denying the others. She even plays favorites with her grandchildren and pits one against the other. One lady I know who has been a typical "Rita" her whole life convinced her husband to make out his will so that the two girls in the family would have a much larger inheritance than the four sons, plus a large income for life, while the sons were forced to share their portion with the girls. The squabble that resulted caused her to disown one of her daughters, and it caused the sons to have bitter feelings toward their sisters after the father passed away.

This elderly lady even delighted in being interviewed by a newspaper reporter (the inheritance was very large and they were a prominent old family in their city) and airing all the dirty linen before the entire population. She has been an embarrassment to her family and has lived a long, contentious life full of wrangling and disagreements. Yet she blames everyone else for her unhappiness.

This type of mother-in-law is a burden to everyone. I have watched the family as they have taken turns doing their "duty" by spending a few hours with her each week, and the only way they have managed is by keeping their sense of humor and reminding themselves that she is to be pitied. Though she may seem exaggerated, I recently read a novel where one of the central characters was a carbon copy of her. As I read, the woman was so familiar to me that I could almost predict her actions. I realized then that I had known many women who had these characteristics, and probably the author had also. They enjoy and even thrive on the trouble they cause. Ironically, they always seem to live quite long lives, possibly because they keep the adrenalin pumping with their familiar ruckuses. (The lady about whom I was speaking is still alive and well at 93.)

However, one has to feel sorry for the type of person who grows old without the love and support of her family because of her own bitterness and morbid desire to cause dissension among them. Eventually the family stops being upset with each other and realizes the cause of it all, and begins to be antagonistic toward the mother. This woman is nearing the end of her life in a huge old house, with hired help to care for her when she could have been surrounded by numerous children, grandchildren, and great-grandchildren. It is truly a sad thing, and undoubtedly a likely ending for all the "Rita Ruckuses" of the world. If you have a mother-in-law who appears to be heading in this direction, she desperately needs your prayers. Her problem is spiritual and emotional. She does not have the stability of Christ as her foundation, and she tries to fill the void by creating diversions—unpleasant ones. Be thankful that you have an example of what not to be in your own life, and ask God to give you His love for her and to help you see her through His eyes. Rita needs every bit of love she can get.

These seven types of mothers-in-law will not fit your own to the letter, but you may find that she is a combination of some or all of them. The pointers listed under "Tenacious Tillie" are ones that will apply to any type of mother-in-law problem. Go over them again, praying to God to show you which of the suggested solutions could best be implemented into your own situation. Knowing that God is in control is helpful because He knew you were going to have that mother-in-law before you were even born. Every person who comes into our lives is a "divine encounter" and will bless us in one of two ways: he or she will be an example either of what we *should* be or of what we should *not* be. If your mother-in-law fits the second category praise God for what He will teach you through her. It will help you to be more sensitive and loving toward your own in-law children when they come along.

6

The Son-in-Law Syndrome

The Problem Son-in-Law

Often a "problem" newlywed in-law is the result
of a poor attitude toward him (or her) by the
mother-in-law. Most young people enter a relationship with their beloved in the hope that they will be
loved and accepted by that person's family. The
marriage survey pointed out that more than half of
the mothers-in-law-to-be treated the prospective
son-in-law or daughter-in-law in a merely polite and
formal manner. However, they did not attempt to
build a relationship and did not change as the couple
became engaged to be married. This is where we
have to take a good look at ourselves and our own
attitudes toward our in-law kids.

It hurts to admit that we have been wrong, but
sometimes we are so busy trying to impress the
one our child has chosen to marry that we forget to
be sensitive to the fact that they want to be *loved* by

us, **not** impressed. If you are already off on the
wrong foot with your son-in-law, there are some
solutions to the problem.

Pray and ask God to show you where you've
been wrong in your relationship to him. Don't try
to make excuses for your actions—just ask God for
His love for your son-in-law. Here are some areas
where you may have fallen short.

1. *Not loving enough*

    Have you treated him as you do your own
    children? Do you attempt to understand
    him? Do you spend as much money on his
    birthday and Christmas gifts as you do your
    own children's? Do you tell him that you ap-
    preciate the way he cares for your daughter?
    Are you interested in his problems and joys
    and his work? Remember to ask God to help
    you see him through His eyes.

2. *Interfering*

    Do you give unasked-for advice? Do you
    visit or call too often? Do you insist on doing
    things your own way?

A young girl in a Bible study I taught came to
me with a problem between her mother and her
husband. Her parents were visiting from another
state, and plans were made for a picnic at the
beach on Saturday. Her husband said they should
be ready to leave at 9:00 A.M., but her mother
thought that was too early. The wife felt her husband was wrong because he insisted on going at
the early hour, while her mother refused to give
in, and followed in a separate car with her own
husband at a much later hour.

The young husband had attempted to explain to his mother-in-law that the level of traffic between our city and the ocean, 30 minutes away, increases greatly on the weekends. There is only one highway to the beach, and it becomes bumper-to-bumper by 10:00 A.M. on Saturdays. Since it crosses a mountain range, cars overheat and it can take up to two hours to make that half-hour drive. The girl's mother was obviously the head of her own household because her father did not even enter the conversation.

When the girl asked me if I didn't think her husband should have surrendered to her mother's wishes, this was my answer: "If my son-in-law said, 'We must get up at 4:00 A.M. and drive to the beach while it is still dark in order to avoid the traffic,' I would be up and ready at 4:00 A.M. and do my best to be cheerful and cooperative. After all, he is the head of his home, and if my visit is to be pleasant, I must respect his wishes."

The girl was surprised, and I asked her if she really desired a marriage such as her mother and father had. She answered that she did not—that she always felt her father was not the leader of his home and that she was glad her husband was not like her father. Make sure you respect your son-in-law's wishes, and make yourself flexible to their life when you are with them.

3. *Critical*

Do you point out your son-in-law's faults to your daughter? This is unforgivable. She will find out his faults on her own, soon enough. Proverbs 17:9 says, "He who covers over an offense promotes love, but whoever repeats the matter separates close friends'' (NIV). You can see how this would apply to a marriage. I know a lady who assisted in the breakup of a marriage by not only agreeing with the wife's criticisms of her husband, but by pointing out additional areas where she thought he was lacking. It would be terribly depressing to have to bear the guilt of contributing to the breakup of one of our children's marriages.

If your daughter complains about her husband, try to counter with his good points and show her that ''nobody's perfect''. Remember, you are hearing only one side of the problem, and there are always at least two sides. Never criticize your son-in-law to his children. That undermines his authority as a father and could result in heartache for the whole family as the children rebel against their father in later years. Don't put him down to your friends, either. When you dwell on his faults, you will see him in a worse light than ever, and Satan will use that to permeate your attitude so that you will have difficulty being loving to him. Philippians 4:8 says to concentrate on the good things in life, and this includes your son-in-law's attributes, however few you may feel there are.

Never side with your grandchildren when your son-in-law punishes them. God has given them the father they need, and if he disciplines them it is because it is necessary. If you feel he is too harsh, pray that God will show him that. God *is* in control and can change the situation completely if He feels it is necessary. Genesis 18:25 says, "Shall not the Judge of all the earth do right?" Only God knows what those children would become if their father did not discipline them.

4. *Resentful*

Do you pout because your son-in-law irritates you? Do you act like a martyr? Are you prone to give him the silent treatment? This is probably more common than being openly hostile. It results in like treatment by the son-in-law. Remember, you catch more flies with honey than with vinegar. A martyr or "poor me" attitude is an extremely poor Christian witness. A joyful person is loved and sought out by everyone, while people shun those who are always feeling sorry for themselves. Whenever we concentrate on our own desires and wishes, we will be unhappy and neglected. When we focus on the needs and desires of our children and involve ourselves with others, we will be like magnets. Nothing attracts others like someone who is sincerely interested in them and who comes across as warm and loving, with a good sense of humor.

Go to your son-in-law privately if your relationship is not what it should be, and apologize for not being the kind of mother-in-law you should have been. Tell him that with God's help you are going to change. Appeal to his male ego. Compliment him and build him up, and he'll think you're wonderful. If he's not affectionate, don't push yourself on him. Hug or kiss him for a gift when he's been away. Eventually he will respond. Compliment him not only to his face, but to others also, including your daughter. And be sincere. If you don't think he has any good points to compliment, ask God to show you.

Show thought in selecting his gifts. Offer to babysit while he and your daughter go out to dinner or for an evening with friends. Also offer to take the children once every few months while they go away overnight or for a weekend. It will spice up their relationship with each other and will give you an opportunity to be closer to your grandchildren. They will be very grateful to you for this. If your son-in-law is having a problem with a job around the house, you and your husband could offer to help him with it. Assist them financially when they really need it, but not to the point where he uses you to bail him out of every problem. If they are young and struggling or if he is trying to finish college or complete a training program, help as much as you can. When our son-in-law was in Bible college studying for the ministry, we sent money to the college directly to apply toward his tuition, which was very expensive and not covered by his G.I. bill.

When a young couple is starting out in married life and has needs, it is often better to supply an item than to give cash. When our daughter found she was pregnant during her husband's senior year at college, she mentioned that they were looking for a secondhand washing machine. (They had been going to the laundromat during his first years in school.) We talked with his parents, and together we split the cost of a washer and dryer for them. We told them to shop around for what they wanted, and when they found a set, to let us know the price and we would send a check. This gave them the pleasure of choosing their own appliances without the burden of the cost. They were able to find a nice set on sale at a chain store, and it gave us the pleasure of providing the gift.

Another mother-in-law I know picks up groceries on sale and takes them to her daughter and son-in-law when she goes to visit them in a nearby town. Sometimes it's paper towels or soap powder and sometimes a beef roast or steaks or fruit that they may not buy for themselves because of the cost. When you have grandchildren it is helpful to buy them shoes or some item that is necessary but costly. Disposable diapers are another item that it is good to provide because it saves your daughter time and prevents the grandbabies from having diaper rash. Ask the Lord to keep you aware of the delicate balance between supportive and taking the responsibility away from your son-in-law. Teach them how to trust God to supply their needs, and don't overindulge them, but if it is within your means to provide them with a luxury now and then, don't hesitate to do it.

I am reminded of a friend of mine whose mother tried to persuade her father to use some of the inheritance he had set aside for the children to install swimming pools for each of them. Both of their children lived in a climate where a pool would be used practically the year round, the grandchildren were all on swim teams, and their son taught swimming at a high school. It was beyond the means of both couples to have their own pool, and the money was simply in the bank awaiting the time when the grandfather would die. He was adamant that he wanted them to have a "decent-sized inheritance," and he would not agree to allowing them the pleasure of having a pool when they would enjoy it most—when their children were at home.

He passed away a couple of years ago, after the grandchildren were grown and married, and the inheritance he so carefully guarded really isn't worth all that much with today's inflation. My friend told me she had learned a lesson from his mistake. She is using her inheritance to help out her own children when they need it most—when they are young and their children are still in their home.

These are suggestions which should help you to have a good relationship with your son-in-law, which in turn will increase the joy in your own life.

If you should happen to have a son-in-law who physically abuses your daughter and/or grandchildren, or who has an alcohol or drug problem, you should insist that he get professional counseling. Be sure that it is with a Christian counselor; a pastor or Christian counseling bureau are most effective and will have a high percentage of lasting results. Do not try to deal with serious problems yourself, and don't let the problem endure until someone is seriously injured. The advice in this book is not intended to solve problems of a crucial nature, but only those which can be rectified by a change in attitude.

7

The Daughter-in-Law Dilemma

The Problem Daughter-in-Law

If I could offer only one piece of advice to the mother of a young man who is getting married, it would be this: *Let go of your son!*

The Bible says in Genesis 2:24 that a man is to LEAVE his father and mother and CLEAVE to his wife. Mom is no longer the number one woman in his life, even though she has a special place in his heart. Recognize that the newlyweds will probably spend more time with *her* parents than with you if you live equally close to them. Expect this and don't be upset about it. She feels more comfortable in her own former home with her own parents, since she doesn't have to be on her best behavior there.

If you make her feel equally welcome, loved, and comfortable in your home, you will also see them often. But if there is even a suspicion of jealousy or a critical spirit toward her, you will be alienating your son as well as his wife. It is up to us as mothers-in-law to see that this does not happen, by giving our own wrong attitudes to God and letting Him change them.

Let me give you an unbelievable, but true, example of a mother-in-law who was everything she was not supposed to be. She was the mother of the husband of a friend of mine. This maladjusted lady was so attached to her son that it was unthinkable to her that he should marry. When he finally decided to wed, in his late twenties, his fiancee's parents lived in another state. This warped lady took outrageous advantage of this young girl, who was my friend.

First, she insisted on being in the wedding party as a bridesmaid! I have never heard of this before or since. She wore a dress of her own choosing—a garish print which did not match the bridesmaid's dresses at all. If there was any sign of opposition to her plans, she would suddenly be stricken with a ''fainting spell'' or her heart would begin to bother her or she would have trouble breathing. She even went on their honeymoon with them (her husband went along with everything she did or said), and they got rooms next door to the newlyweds in their hotel.

When they set up housekeeping, the mother-in-law visited constantly and criticized the young girl until she was a nervous wreck. When their son was born, his grandmother named him without consulting his mother, and took over almost his complete care afterward. My friend, finally, on the advice of her doctor, told her husband he would have to move her away from his mother's domineering presence, as she could no longer live under such tension. He flatly refused, and when his mother said he would have to choose between her and his wife, he chose his mother and divorced his wife. She was a strong Catholic girl, and the whole situation was so traumatic that it took her years to recover from it. This seems a very exaggerated case, but I am sure there are other instances similar to it. It is a sad commentary about a mother who would not "let go."

Following are some pointers in building a relationship with your daughter-in-law.

1. We should always, as mothers-in-law, be unselfishly concerned with our daughter-in-law's happiness.

Her frame of mind and contentment is responsible for our son's happiness, and we would not want to do anything to jeopardize either of them.

2. As with any of our in-law kids, we must *never* criticize his wife to him.

If we do criticize, we run the risk of pointing out faults he wouldn't notice, thereby causing him to be dissatisfied with his marriage. If you see areas where she is seriously failing, pray about them. DON'T go to her and tell her; you will alienate her and hurt her feelings. Remember your own first years as a bride. Were you the perfect wife?

I certainly couldn't have passed my examination on the qualities of homemaking. I was a terrible cook! My husband still jokes about the first chicken pie I made. He stuck his fork into it and the whole pie lifted off the plate, it was so gummy! I washed the dark clothes with the white, getting lint all over both. We went on vacation and I unplugged the refrigerator and left the door closed. (That was a *real* homecoming for us!) I lost a half-month's paycheck and we had to wait three months for a duplicate money order. I tried to sew on a button and sewed it to the back of his shirt. I drove over a log in a parking lot with our new car. I forgot to mail the telephone bill and our phone was disconnected. In view of all this, I couldn't possibly be a very critical mother-in-law, could I? Anyone can think of countless blunders she has made during her own years as a wife.

If you criticize your daughter-in-law to your son,you will alienate him. My grandmother, poor lady, was an example of this. Apparently she had it in her mind for my uncle to marry a neighbor he dated, and when he chose someone else, Grandma just could not accept her. His choice was superior, and a more lovely lady he could not have found. She was a good cook and housekeeper, she loved him devotedly, and he often told me he was the happiest man on earth. However, my grandmother treated his wife so coldly that she finally stopped coming to his parents' home at all. My grandfather never became friendly to her during her entire lifetime. Consequently, she rarely saw my uncle, since he would not come to visit for any length of time without his wife. I think of all the sweet fellowship that my grandmother missed with this marvelous Christian lady. When my uncle passed away at 45, she never remarried. We love her very much and feel sorry for all she suffered as a result of another possessive mother.

3. Be sure never to criticize your daughter-in-law's parents to your son.

If they are good in-laws and he loves them, he will think you are jealous and tend to spend more time with them. If they are not good in-laws, you will only add fuel to the fire and make him more dissatisfied, and it will be harder for him to get along with them. It may even cause problems between him and his wife and jeopardize the relationship between you and her family. She will probably tell her mother and father what you have said, and you could end up estranged. ''Feudin', fussin', and fightin''' belong back in the early century with the Hatfields and the McCoys, and certainly not in the life of a Christian.

A lady in my Bible study told me how sad each holiday has become because her family and her husband's family are not speaking to each other. They were unable to celebrate their children's birthdays together and had to have two separate parties; Christmas had to be divided, and if one set of grandparents attended a function at school (or a Little League game or a dance recital), the other set would not be present. She said she couldn't imagine what they would do when the kids grew up and married—they certainly couldn't put-on two weddings for each child. It's inconceivable that adults could act so childishly—and imagine the example they are setting for their grandchildren!

4. Encourage your son to take the lead in his family, both spiritually and emotionally.

Suggest that he pray with his wife, and remind him to be thoughtful. When our second son, Jay, was married, he happened to call us shortly before he had been married a month. I asked him what he was going to get his wife, Debbie, for their "month anniversary." He replied that he hadn't even thought about celebrating it. I suggested that he buy a small gift and make a fuss over the date, and that this would please her. He thanked me and said he would do so, and he appreciated my telling him about it. Otherwise he would not have known that it might be expected of him.

5. Do thoughtful, helpful things for your daughter-in- law.

Drop by with some yummy fruit for her; loan her books if she likes to read, and your magazines when you finish them (if she does not subscribe to them). Offer to babysit so she can have a day by herself.

6. If your relationship is not good, restore it by apologizing to her and asking God to help you to be closer to her.

7. Be grateful for her—that she loves your son and grandchildren.

8. Don't try to take her own mother's place, but be a good, kind friend to her.

9. Listen to her opinions but don't try to force yours on her.

10. Don't give her unasked-for advice on raising her kids.

11 *Never* criticize her to her children.

12. Don't criticize her to your friends.

Criticizing her will make you more unhappy with her, which will cause bitterness between you. It may get back to her and hurt her deeply. Your friends will carry an offense for you and dislike her. It will magnify her faults as you discuss them with others. It causes you to dwell on them instead of on her good points.

13. Give her small gifts and cards occasionally—a book, a scarf, flowers, or something you have made.

14. Develop your sense of humor and be understanding.

Think back, as I did, to when you were first married and weren't a talented cook and housekeeper; we tend to overlook our own faults and concentrate on someone else's. If she isn't helpful when she comes to visit, either her mother hasn't trained her to be (so it's not her fault) or she doesn't know how and is afraid of doing something wrong. Both of these were true in my case—my mom didn't teach me how to do anything in the home, as she was a perfectionist and preferred to do it herself. Therefore I didn't know how to be helpful to others, and I ended up doing things wrong. Don't be afraid to ask for her help with the dishes or cooking—she will appreciate it and feel more comfortable.

15. Pray for your daughter-in-law faithfully. This will give your relationship a depth you could never have thought possible. If she is a Christian (hopefully she is), consider how fortunate you are. You can pray with her and have the kind of communication that isn't possible between non-Christians. God can overcome any obstacle (Luke 1:37), and you have an obligation as a mature Christian to have a special and loving bond between yourself and the young woman who loves your son even more than you do.

8

Shirttail Relations

The Other In-Laws

If you have an average-sized family (two to four children), you will end up with that many "extra" families that are what is commonly referred to as "shirttail" relations. If they do not live in the same area, your contact with them may be an occasional letter, a Christmas card, or an evening out with them when they are visiting your children. If they do live in your town, however, you need to develop a livable relationship with them. It isn't always possible to be close friends in that you may not share the same interests, you may be busy with your other friends and activities, or you may not be comfortable with each other's lifestyles. If they happen to be non-Christians, this will probably be the case. It is, however, possible to develop the type of relationship that will make the children comfortable when you need to get together and that will not cause problems if they choose to spend a holiday with the other in-laws.

We have seen all degrees of relationships with in-laws. We attended a wedding one time where it was obvious that neither family was speaking to the other, and we have known in-laws who were best friends. Most of us, however, fit somewhere between these two extremes.

The best advice I can give on getting along with your children's in-laws is to follow the Golden Rule. Treat them as you would like to be treated and as Jesus would want you to behave toward them. We should be loving, giving, sharing, flexible, and patient with their idiosyncrasies, and we should *never* criticize them to our children. If your son's mother-in-law insists that they spend *every* holiday with her family, accept it cheerfully and expect God to give you the grace to do so. Don't put pressure on your children that will cause them to feel guilty or have a disagreement with the other family.

As you give in to them with the right attitude, you will endear yourselves to your children and will find that they spend more time with you in the long run. (Unless, of course, the reason they spend more time with the other in-laws is that they are **less** demanding, more fun to be with, and more loving to the couple. We need to search ourselves and ask God to reveal to us areas where we need to improve as in-laws.

Most young couples are pretty sensitive about spending alternate holidays with parents and not leaving anyone out. You may find that you will be more likely to see your daughters on holidays than your sons, as girls tend to cling more to their mothers. If your daughters-in-law feel comfortable in your home and you make them welcome and love them, there should be no problem.

It is nice to include your child's in-laws at family gatherings and for holidays. This will be easier when there is only one married child. As each one takes on a whole new set of relatives, it becomes impossible due to the size and varied interests to get everyone together for anything short of a wedding, baptism, or funeral. We spent holidays with our oldest son's in-laws, even after he was killed, until his wife's mother passed away and her father remarried. Then when our daughter was married and both of our other sons were still single, we got together with all of her in-laws, for each holiday.

However, after our sons married, it was impossible to include each of their wives' parents, plus brothers and sisters and spouses, so we remain flexible as to holidays at this point. We offer to have dinner at our home, and if any of them can come, they do. If they are unable to come, however, we always receive an invitation to their homes or to their in-law's homes, so we try not to make definite plans or hold fast to traditions. As they marry and have their own families, they want to establish their own traditions, and those we had are no longer fitting. Probably one of the main causes of problems during the holidays results from a mother and father who refuse to give up their family traditions and try to force their children into the same mold they were in while growing up.

For instance, we always spent holidays (especially Christmas) at our "mountain house." We cut down a big cedar tree, and on Christmas eve we would have clam chowder, build a fire, read Scripture, share, and sing Christmas carols. Then around 11:00 P.M. we would open our gifts. We slept in on Christmas morning and had a big turkey dinner, inviting anyone we knew who didn't have a place to go.

We all loved and enjoyed this tradition, but as the children married it had to be changed. All of our children's relatives live in the Bay Area of California (as we do), and it would be impossible to continue our habit of going to the Sierras for Christmas and be able to include the other relatives in on the holiday. We now have Christmas eve at our daughter's home, and whoever can make it joins us. Christmas dinner is the same way—she and her husband are establishing their own traditions with their children, and we join them. When our other boys have children, we will probably alternate where we spend the holidays each year, but we are flexible, allowing them to do as they wish in their own homes without fear of offending us. I'm sure that none of them would allow us to spend the holidays alone, and we are on good terms with all of the in-laws so that we could get together with any of them for a holiday and enjoy it.

The point is that we all need to get to the place of realizing that our children who are married now have their own family unit and that we must give up our own traditional customs to follow their ways. The important thing is that everyone should enjoy holidays without family fights, hurt feelings, or unpleasantness of any kind. It is up to us as Christians to set a good example for our children so they can pass it on to their own family.

What if you have tried your hardest to be flexible, loving, and warm toward your married child's in-laws, and they either do not respond or are antagonistic toward you? If you can honestly, before the Lord, say that you have made every attempt to get along well, then it is *their* problem, not yours, and a matter for concerned, diligent prayer. Perhaps you unknowingly offended them at some time, or it is possible that your children prefer your company to theirs, and there is jealousy. It is also likely that if you are a Christian and they don't share your beliefs, they may be antagonistic to them and to your standards.

I overheard a lady speaking to her friend about the parent of her son's fiancee. She was saying that they didn't drink and didn't want to have a champagne reception, and how upset that made her. I felt sorry for the girl's parents, even though I didn't know them, because I could see trouble ahead for them trying to keep peace with the new in-laws. The woman made several disparaging remarks about "church people" and the disadvantages of having them in the family.

If you should be unfortunate and find yourself with shirttail relatives such as this woman, it is going to take much prayer, grace, and forgiveness to get along with them. I can only suggest being as loving as possible and never having a judgmental, critical attitude toward them. If you disapprove of some of their habits, just remember that "there but for the grace of God" could be you. Overlook the things which displease you, and concentrate on what is good about the family. Just think of all the lessons in patience the Lord will teach you through them! As my husband always says, "It makes you appreciate all the nice people you meet when you have to bear the burden of someone who is hard to get along with."

The important thing is for you to keep your relationship with the Lord in order and to respond to the situation in His way. This is a good time to put into action what we like to call your "R & R" time. The first "R" is for "reaction" and the second is for "recovery." If the in-law makes a critical remark to you, the time between your reaction of hurt or anger and your recovery, where you accept the remark as from the Lord and under His control, is a measure of your spiritual maturity. If you react unfavorably and say something critical in return, you need to give the problem to the Lord and let Him take care of it. If you are able to control your immediate response and recover quickly with a kind retort (remember, "a gentle answer turns away wrath"—Proverbs 15:1 NIV), then your level of spirituality is where it should be.

Each person whom God allows to come into your life is there to teach us a lesson, and God uses these lessons to mold us into the kind of people He wants us to be. For this reason we can praise Him for those relatives who seem to be a burden rather than a blessing. It's all part of His perfect plan, and He will give us the grace and wisdom to learn from it. No matter how bad you think your "shirt-tail" in-laws are, they could be worse! Hopefully, as you put these principles into practice, they will become your good friends.

9

Faraway Places

The Out-of-Town Children

If your married children live in another city or
state, your chances of having problems with them
are minimized, but on the other hand, so are your
joys. I agree with Bill Gothard that it is ever so
much nicer when families can live within visiting
proximity to each other. In our mobile society today, we see cases of families who get together once
every five to ten years and do not keep in touch
except when there is a birth, death, or marriage.

We are fortunate to have one son and daughter-
in-law and our oldest son's widow, their son, and
her husband and daughter in the same city. Our
daughter and her family live in a small town 20
miles away. Our second son and his wife are about
a four-hour drive from us. We see the ones close
by weekly, and keep in touch that often with Jay
and Debbie by telephone. We plan weekends at

the mountain house periodically and try to get together for holidays several times a year.

If your children live a long distance from you, we would suggest that you make it a point to see them as often as possible. One of the greatest pleasures in life is seeing your children happy and secure in their own homes, and getting to know your grandchildren. Your influence on their lives is irreplaceable, and grandparents often lead their grandchildren to the Lord and influence them to lead godly lives.

I had the privilege of praying with our oldest grandson, Clint, to receive Christ into his heart at the age of six, and of seeing him baptized in our swimming pool by his pastor uncle when he was nine years old. His grandfather and I read the Bible with him each Monday night when he comes for dinner and to spend the night. We pray for him daily, as we do for all our children and grandchildren, and my husband provided a father image for him after his own father was killed in Vietnam. His mother remarried after ten years, but during that time we were able to build a relationship with Clint that has had a profound effect on his life.

Too often families don't make the effort to see each other often because of expense or inconvenience, but will spend the money to attend the funeral after a family member dies. We learned that lesson the hard way when our nephew in another state was killed. We had tried to get together with my husband's brother and family at least every other year, but when Ron was killed, we made it a point to get together at least once a year even though they live

1000 miles from us. We decided that since none of us knows how long we have on this earth, we want to take advantage of the time to be close as a family and to have our children know each other. When our daughter and her husband lived in another state while he attended college, we would fly to see them on a long weekend, meet them halfway to go camping during the summer, fly them home on special occasions, and make the long drive a couple of times a year besides.

We have never regretted any of the money spent on getting together, and it has made our relationship closer because we made the effort. We try to attend all the nieces' and nephews' and cousins' weddings, as they are joyous occasions. We know how we appreciated our families' journeying from faraway places to attend the weddings of our children. Sometimes it is impossible to attend them, but we try our best.

Getting together if your children live far away may require more sacrifice on your part financially, but you are undoubtedly more able to do it than they are while raising their family. Our daughter's in-laws travel halfway across the country each year to see their daughter and her family, and we know of others who make even longer journeys. Family ties are important, and we need to take precaution that they don't come untied through neglect or carelessness.

When my grandmother was young, her family settled in different areas, and by the time she was in her forties they had completely lost track of her brother who moved to California. Communication was much more difficult in those days, and one didn't telephone long-distance unless someone died or was born. Long automobile trips were a nightmare because of the undependability of the cars and road conditions.

But today we have no excuse not to keep in close contact, now with the off-hour telephone rates and the discount airplane flights. If we teach our children to get along well and to love each other as they are growing up, they will be more likely to keep in contact their whole lives. And if we set the example of keeping in touch with them often, they will want to do the same with their own children as they grow up.

If both sets of in-laws live in the same area while their children live a distance away, an auto trip to visit them can be made at half-price by splitting the expenses. Sometimes we may prefer to visit alone and not share the time with someone else, but extra visits are fun when taken with another couple.

There is one advantage to having children live in another town where you can spend a few days with them: you get to know them much better when you are staying at their home. We feel closer to our son-in-law since we stayed at their home so often while he was in college, 600 miles from us. This can work in the opposite way, of course, if you are not careful to be undemanding and flexible as to their plans. If their home is very cramped (such as an apartment), it would possibly be better to offer to stay at a motel while visiting. If they are insistent that you stay with them, however, do so.

Sometimes I feel we have gotten too used to

creature comforts and must have our own bedroom and bath when we visit relatives. I can remember going to my aunt and uncle's small farmhouse in Washington State as a child. We slept on the floor, on camp cots, on the sofa, and even outside when the weather permitted, and it was such fun. A friend of mine tells of visiting an aunt who had several children, and the kids would sleep three or four in a bed, crossways, and had a ball! We slept on the hide-a-bed in our daughter's living room and shared their bathroom and got along fine. You really get to know one another while waiting in line for the bathroom in wrinkled nightgown, uncombed hair, and unbrushed teeth!

If your children are visiting in your town, be sure not to be overly demanding of their time. If they have other in-laws in the same area, share and share alike, and include them in your get-togethers. They will want to see their friends too, so be generous in allowing them to arrange their own schedule to spend time with those to whom they are close. One young couple whom we know stopped spending their vacations in their hometown because their parents fought over who got to see more of them and resented the time they spent with other friends. If the other in-laws are not Christians, you may even have to bend over backwards and give up some of your time with your own children in order to keep peace, but the Lord will reward you for this by giving you other opportunities to see them. It will also make them more aware of the difference between Christian and unbelieving in-laws.

As to the length of visit when you go to be with

them, you can determine this by how much fun all of you have. We found that four or five days was perfect, and even a week wasn't too long, but I believe any longer than that could be a burden. Sometimes it is necessary to stay longer because of the distance traveled to get there, or in the case of a new baby's arrival and the need for your help. If you must travel all the way across the country, try to spend a few days with the couple, then maybe a few days sightseeing, and a few more days with your children before leaving. This will break up your visit and take the pressure off them. Be sure to help with the housework and with the purchase of groceries, and take them out to dinner if possible. Some in-laws visit and expect to be treated like guests, not like family. It's important to make the couple feel as relaxed as possible during your visit.

There are many creative ways to work out visits with your children without making them feel that it is a trial to have you as guests. The most important thing is your attitude toward them and being casual about meals, where you sleep, and what you do. They may want to show you the sights, but don't make them feel pressured to perform taxi service in squiring you from one place to another each day. It will be a burden to them. Your primary reason for visiting is to build your relationship with the young couple, and if you keep this in mind, just being together will make the occasion memorable.

10

The Counselor's Couch

When Marital Problems Arise

On July 22, 1980, we were flying from Seattle to California after visiting with friends and relatives. Suddenly our plane made a sharp detour to the right and the pilot's voice announced, "Ladies and gentlemen, Mount St. Helens erupted again. We are detouring around the ash cloud, and if you will look out the right side of the aircraft, you will have a once-in-a-lifetime view." As we watched the enormous black cloud belching from the mountaintop, it was an awesome sight. The mushroom head of the cloud was at 22,000 feet by that time and our plane was at 18,000 feet. It was indeed overwhelming to watch the once-beautiful mountain, now barren of snow and trees, sending forth a cloud that would cover much of the state of Washington, drop its ashes on Idaho, and Montana, and sprinkle Canada on its way to the East coast.

I remembered Mount St. Helens when I had seen it from Portland when visiting that city. It had been beautiful—snowcapped and peaceful against the sky. It remained so for years, but during the past few months there were earthquakes and internal rumblings, then puffs of steam, and finally in May 1980, it blew its top, killing many people and making desolate thousands of acres of magnificent country.

This transformation is a picture of what happens in some marriages. Everything seems peaceful and serene. Then there are a few ripples on the surface which no one takes too seriously, just as those who were camping on Mount St. Helens thought there was no real danger. Suddenly the top blows, devastating everything in sight. These are the marriages that surprise us completely when they break up, while those neighbors or friends who have been arguing and fighting for years are still together. What happens to the ''perfect'' marriages while the obviously troubled ones seem to hang in there?

The marriages we thought were good have been simmering beneath the surface and more unhappy for the participants than the ones where the couple got their troubles into the open. When we are aware of a problem and discussing it, the first steps toward solving it have been taken. When it is buried it will never be solved, and the next crisis only adds to it. Finally, like St. Helens, it blows up! Those who discuss their differences seldom suffer from ulcers, hypertension, or colitus, as do those who refuse to acknowledge the problem and turn their backs on it.

I am reminded of the seemingly fantastic marriage of Anita Bryant and Bob Greene. I recall reading her books and thinking how fortunate she was to have such a "made-in-heaven" life. Yet she shocked the whole world by telling everyone how unhappy she had been for years and had been "acting" a part until she too blew her top and sued for divorce.

As mothers-in-law, we can be sure our children will experience times in their marriages when they are angry, disappointed, hurt, or frustrated because of the actions of their mates. Hopefully these problems will be so minor that they will not even bother to share them with us. But if they do share them or they seem to be developing into a serious disagreement, what is our role? Do we ever take sides or try to resolve the problem ourselves? I believe we should always remain objective and *never* take sides. Probably we will only hear one side of the problem—that of our own child. Never forget that there are *two* sides to every argument, no matter how it is presented to us. Don't make a judgment until you hear the other side. Proverbs 18:17 says: "The first to present his case seems right, till another comes forward and questions him" (NIV).

I am reminded of a couple who was counseling a young woman who had terrible tales to tell about the way her husband treated her. He took away her car keys so she couldn't even drive to the grocery store; he checked up on her during the day by telephone; he would not allow her to go anyplace alone. The people who were counseling her made an appointment with the husband to find out why he was so unreasonable to his wife. They were shocked to learn that the reason he took her car keys and was so strict with her was that she was using her car to meet her boyfriend while her husband was at work. The husband was doing his best to end the relationship and force his wife to stay home with their children. There were definitely two sides to that story!

As a mother-in-law, you are not likely to be able to hear both sides of an argument between your child and his mate. This is why it is best to try to discern, through prayer and listening carefully, what the root problem might be and not form any judgment in the matter. Sometimes we can detect a wrong attitude or action just by asking the Lord to help us see what the problem is. It is very difficult, however, not to take the side of our own child. We have been defending them their entire lives and possibly even making excuses for them. Now that they are grown and married, it is time for them to assume responsibility for their own actions. It helps to know some of the basic causes of quarrels and the attitudes that result in disagreements. Just remember: don't choose sides; be as objective as possible!

We will attempt to go into some of the more common causes of disagreements in marriage so that you might be able to discern wrong responses or attitudes that your own child might have when coming to you for advice. The four top causes of marital problems are: 1) communication, 2) disciplining of children, 3) a home out of order, and 4) money.

Communicating seems to be the number one cause of difficulty in a marriage, according to a survey I took at a number of seminars and Bible studies a few years ago. As a result, I wrote *Put Love in Your Marriage,* which is a book on communication. Conversation seems to be somewhat of a lost art, due in large part to what is commonly called "the boob tube." Families sit mesmerized before their favorite programs, not speaking to each other or sharing. In fact, if someone tries to talk, he is often hushed unless it is during a commercial.

If you see your own offspring's family too involved with TV, you might try mentioning it to your son or daughter (*not* the in-law) *once* only. If the reaction is negative or resentful, don't bring the matter up again. Just pray about it! You'd be surprised what God can do when you don't try to help Him out. I have truly found this to be the most effective way of dealing with any potential or existing problem in the lives of my married children. We can suggest, manipulate, hint, nag, and push to no avail, while conscientious prayer will accomplish wonders.

Many times young couples will resent advice because it makes them feel insecure in making their own decisions. Mom and dad have been in on their choices for so long that now they want to be on their own. If you think your suggestion will not be welcome, it's better not to make it at all, but instead go directly to the Lord in prayer. James 5:16 says, "The prayer of a righteous man is powerful and effective." (NIV). I have also claimed Proverbs 21:1—"The king's heart is in the hand of the Lord; He directs it like a water-course wherever He pleases'' (NIV). God can change anyone's mind, and it is much easier on your relationship with your married children if God changes their minds without your help. They believe it to be their own idea, or from the Lord, and they don't lose face that way.

There are many excellent books on communication, and if you have established good rapport with your child, he will attempt to do so in his family. Usually the complainer is the one who shares, while the ''complained-about'' does not. If your child is seeking your advice, it will probably be because his mate does not communicate well. Your job will be to encourage your own child to try harder to please his partner, to share deeply from his own life, and to treat the shy mate with such tenderness that she will not be afraid of being hurt. Don't ever join in his complaints or you will make him more dissatisfied and cause real problems in the marriage. Offer creative suggestions in solving the problem. Encourage him to pray with his wife and to take their communication problem to the Lord. If it seems extremely serious, suggest that they discuss it with their pastor.

Offer to care for their children so they can get away together for a few days. Often this is the answer to a lack of understanding between them. Couples become so busy with activities and work and children that they do not have the time to just sit down and talk. If you do not live in the same town, offer to come for a weekend and visit with the children while they take the time away as a "mini-moon." ("Mini-moons" are short, honeymoon-type vacations which need to be taken periodically to revitalize a marriage.)

The second problem, that of child discipline, is a very touchy one. Grandmas are notorious for being overly lenient with their grandchildren. It is best if you can maintain pretty much the same standards that the parents have when the children are visiting you. If, however, there is no discipline in the home, it is well to speak lovingly but firmly to your son or daughter, suggesting that they read in the Book of Proverbs the standards of God's discipline. Dr. James Dobson's books *Dare to Discipline* and *The Strong-Willed Child* are excellent and worthwhile to give to your children.

It is particularly important to do this while they are still very young, before the problems get out of hand. If they seem to be too harsh with the children, slapping them in the face or punishing them far beyond the crime, you had better use your knees instead of your mouth. In the case of overdiscipline, there is usually a bad temper involved with one or both of the parents, and your suggestions would only be interpreted as interference. In the case of child abuse, of course, the authorities must be notified, and professional counseling is needed.

If the grandchildren are causing problems in your children's marriage because of their lack of discipline and rebellion, you can be supportive of the parents and as influential as you can be with the young people. I have seen a case where a rebellious two-year-old almost destroyed a marriage because it was impossible for either the mother or father to enjoy themselves when the child was not in bed. They were unable to have company or visit anyone without the child causing such a disturbance that the time was ruined for everyone. He would destroy knickknacks, kick at his parents, scream, and throw tantrums. It was clearly a case of the father falling down on his job as head of the house. The mother yelled at the little boy constantly but did not punish him, and the father ignored the whole situation.

The problem was finally solved after the arrival of another baby. The father was forced to assume some of the care of the two-year-old while the mother was busy with the new baby, and he began punishing the little guy for his disobedience. This was all the child wanted, anyway—proof of their love as they set limits for his actions.and his response was to shape up!

The home out of order probably results in more divorces and more rebellious children than any other problem. If it is your daughter's home, you must encourage her to step down from the lead and allow her husband to assume his rightful position. *The Fulfilled Woman* goes into great detail on how to get the home back into its proper perspective.

A man can't lead if there is no one to follow, so it is generally easier for the woman to get her act together and her house in order. The Bible says, "The wise woman builds her house, but with her own hands the foolish one tears hers down" (Proverbs 14:1 NIV). The wife sets the tone of the home because it is her domain. She usually chooses the furnishings and color schemes, and it is up to her whether it is a "house" or a "home." The dictionary defines a "house" as "a building in which people live," but the definition of a home is "a place of refuge where people can rest and be safe." Quite a difference!

Hopefully, your own home is in order and your daughter will have a good example to follow. The husband should discuss plans with his wife, but the final decision should be up to him. She should allow him to function in the role God intended for him, with her full support. Remember that God speaks to wives through their husbands, and if we are disobeying our husbands, we are really disobeying God. Our mate is our umbrella of protection, and God can't protect us if we are out from under the umbrella. Raindrops (and everything else) are going to be falling on our heads.

Submission has become a "dirty word" among women these days, particularly those involved with ERA. I heard an amusing definition of the word "submission" during a seminar at church last winter. The man leading the conference said, "Submission is learning to duck so God can hit your husband!" If women would think of it in this way, it would be easier to submit. I, for one, am afraid to be out of God's will by disobeying my husband because whatever results because of my stubbornness is my responsibility, not his! Even if he makes a wrong decision, it is God's will for us as a family, and He will overrule if He chooses. It is a very comfortable, secure feeling for me not to have to make final decisions or take the responsibility that might mean the difference between security or failure for my family.

A role reversal in the home nearly always results in rebellious children. The sons lose respect for their fathers and have a poor relationship with their mothers and a lack of respect for authority in general. They may even dislike females for a time and will tend to date very mousy, quiet girls. Daughters in such a family will often show disdain for men and may even end up unhappily married because of a poor father-image. I personally know of a family where the mother was definitely head of the house, and two of the three daughters became lesbians. Their disrespect for their father was evident during their growing-up years, and they were never able to have a normal relationship with the opposite sex.

As in every other area, the best teaching we can give to our children in their own marriages is by our example. If our own marriages are in order, usually theirs will be too. If we have failed in some areas, it is not too late to make a fresh start and allow them to see the success we have in improving our relationship with our husband.

The fourth cause of marital problems, money, is probably even more pertinent today than ever. With the enormous inflation we are experiencing, few people have enough money to meet their obligations without the wife working or the husband moonlighting.

I personally have been fortunate in not having had to work outside my home since my helping my husband finish college the first two years of our marriage. We had four children, and I was always able to be at home to meet their needs, get to know their friends, and spend time making our house a "home," with time left over to be involved in our church. As the children were grown, God has blessed me by giving me the ability to write, teach, and speak to women in many parts of the country and in my own church. If I had it to do over again, I would stay home with my children just as I did and would certainly live in a very modest home if I needed to in order to raise my own family. (We lived in some pretty modest homes, too, including the one with the plywood floors.)

I realize that some women must work in order to put food on the table and pay the electric bill, but those who are working in order to have a beautiful home, nicer cars, exciting vacations, and other material things at the expense of their children may be sorry someday. Children grow up and are gone very quickly, and if you've never had time to establish a good relationship with them, you may be in for a lonely old age.

Recently our daughter and son-in-law decided to move out of their expensive home and build a smaller house where the payments would be less and they would have the money to enjoy doing things with their children more often. They were entirely convinced that they were choosing wisely after counseling with a middle-aged couple in their church who had made the opposite choice. They had decided, when their children were young, that it was important for them to have as many material advantages as possible. Although the husband had a prestigious position, his salary was only a little above average. The decision was made for the wife to resume her career in order to provide for a large, beautifully decorated home as well as extra material possessions for the children.

At the time our daughter and her husband were discussing their own decision with the couple, this is the advice they gave them: "It isn't worth it to work and put your money into an elaborate home. Kids don't really care that much, and the time you sacrifice that you can't spend with them can never be regained. Our children are now grown, and we look back at all the things we didn't do because we were too tired from putting all our energies into giving them things and didn't have the time to go camping, go to Disneyland, stay up late and talk to them, play games, and just be parents. It makes us sad, and believe us, if we could go back and relive our lives, we would put first things first. We would have a more modest home, we would have a normal family life with a mother at home spending time with her children and friends, and we wouldn't have missed it all."

This couple was adamant in their views of the unimportance of the material possessions they strove so hard to provide for their family. The intangibles—the time spent just being together without pressure and the absence of the divided heart between job, home, and children—were something they had never had, and they would now give anything to regain it. My daughter-in-law who is a teacher (and who intends to resign as soon as she has a baby) recently told me that she had never yet met one high-school student whose mother worked, who didn't wish that someone would be home when they arrived from school.

If you have given your own children the proper values in life and de-emphasized what the world considers success, they aren't going to have serious disagreements over money, the lack of it, or how to spend it. If they are having financial problems and are seriously trying to get that area of their lives in order, do help out if you can. If you can help by providing some of their needs so that your grandchildren will have their mother at home, it will be one of the most rewarding services you've ever performed. No one else can give the children the love and security provided by their own mother, and I don't know of any nursery school or baby-sitter who can take her place.

There are many other factors prevalent in marital problems—the use of free time, different tastes, alcoholism, sexual problems, etc., and we do not have space to go into all of these here. We would encourage professional counseling in all serious problems. Do not attempt to deal with them yourself except to step in where there is physical abuse. It is impossible for a parent to give completely objective, unbiased marital counseling. He or she is too close to the problem to detach himself emotionally from it, yet this is what needs to be done in order to give effective advice.

Urge your child and his or her mate to seek the help of their pastor or other Christian counselor, and then pray for them. The less involved you are personally, the more comfortable the couple will feel around you and the more supportive you can be. Your prayers are so much more valuable than your advice! If you can remember this when there seems to be trouble brewing, you will be allowing God to work in a special way in your married children's lives and perhaps prevent a "Mount St. Helens" explosion.

11

The Solo In-Law

The Widowed or Divorced Mother-in-Law

"But if a widow has children or grandchildren, these should learn first of all to put their religion into practice by caring for their own family and so repaying their parents and grandparents, for this is pleasing to God." (1 Timothy 5:4 NIV). Verse 8 says, "If anyone does not provide for his relatives, and especially for his immediate family, he has denied the faith and is worse than an unbeliever" (NIV).

Does this mean that if our mother-in-law is widowed or divorced, she should move into our home and we should fully support her financially? Chapter 5 of 1 Timothy makes it clear that there are extenuating circumstances. It depends upon the age and financial status of the widow or divorcee. There is apparently a "list" for widows who have no family to care for them, and these are evidently the responsibility of the church.

As usual, the Bible stresses common sense in these situations. If a widow is financially independent, has a job or career, and is able to care for herself, it seems logical that she should do so. If, however, she is ill or in need of support, her family should come to her aid. If the family is unable to support her fully, we have means through our states to help out with her care. It is most important to make sure that she is given the love and emotional support she needs, and everyone can do this.

If you have a widowed or divorced mother or mother-in-law, you may enjoy having her as part of your household, particularly if she is a Christian and your personalities are compatible. By this, we mean that each of you is willing to make the adjustments necessary for harmonious blending of two households. She should be given time to recover from her grief at being alone, of course, but she will need to realize that she is no longer responsible for the decisions made in the household and must adapt to your family lifestyle.

You in turn should make allowances for the traumatic experience through which she is going, remembering that you may have such a fate in store for you someday. She should not be treated as a servant or built-in baby-sitter, but as an independent member of the family. If she is a Christian, she will find great comfort in being involved in her church and will undoubtedly be busy with service and social activities in that area.

If your mother or mother-in-law is accustomed to working and has a job or career which she enjoys, it may be better for all concerned if she does not make any major decisions for a time. A period of adjustment is easier when there are fewer adaptations to make. Don't rush her out of her home or insist that she move many miles away to your home. She will be happier surrounded by friends and familiar objects for a while. Later she may find that the memories are too painful and may wish to relocate.

We found this to be true after our oldest son was killed in Vietnam. We had just purchased some property in the Sierras near Yosemite National Park, and we went ahead with the building of a second home there. It was marvelous therapy for my husband to do the finishing work on the house, and it saved our sanity at Christmastime to be able to spend the holidays in a place which contained no memories at all and had completely different surroundings. Many widows have told me that after a few months or a year in their homes, they have decided to relocate because the constant memories were very depressing to them. Many moved either into condominiums or mobile home parks, the latter seeming to be more satisfactory because of the more friendly atmosphere and the number of people in the same predicament.

When a mother or mother-in-law is not a Christian, it may be a strain on your relationship to have her in your home, and if other arrangements can be worked out, we would suggest that this be done. Our experience with the problem was not good, and we have known many others who have had the same problems we did. When my stepfather passed away, my mother was in her midfifties. I should explain that I was adopted (although I didn't learn this until after my mother died), and I lived with various relatives while I was growing up. My mother and stepfather lived in Seattle, and we had been living in California for years due to a business transfer. We immediately invited my mother to move into our home, and we built an addition of two rooms for her. She spent the first couple of years living our lives vicariously. She had worked most of her life and now was at loose ends with no job, her good friends and other relatives in another state, and little patience with a houseful of lively children. Our lifestyle was considerably more casual than what she was used to, and it was very difficult for all of us.

Finally she decided to go back to work, and that was an improvement. However, an additional burden was placed on me in caring for seven people and a large home and bearing the criticism of another woman who was used to a quiet, well-ordered, immaculate home with only occasional guests. Our house was like Grand Central Station, according to my mother, and it was very difficult to her to adjust to the noise, confusion, and constant company.

Eventually, after four years, my mother decided that an apartment of her own was the answer, and she moved to a complex where several of her co-workers lived. We were all much happier and our relationship improved considerably. She came to dinner often and was free to relax in her own home when work was over. She built a pleasant life for herself, taking vacations with her friends and joining them for dinner, but still having her family close by.

Her beautiful Christian landlady led her to the Lord and she became active in her church, which also made a big difference in our relationship.

Later on, when she was nearly 70, she had a slight stroke and spent several months recuperating in the hospital and at our home. She was able to go back into her own apartment after her therapy was completed, although eventually she moved closer to our home, where I could look in on her often. When she was in her late seventies, she had a more serious stroke and lost her ability to walk. After a time in the hospital, the doctor recommended that she go to a convalescent hospital a couple of miles from us, where she could have the 24-hour care she needed. She had grown quite heavy from her inactivity, and since I am just over five feet tall, I could not lift her in order to care for her personal needs.

I have heard many horror stories about convalescent homes, but other than a few people who are mentally disabled through illness, they do provide the answer for a situation such as ours was. There were many bright, alert people living there, as well as many who were young but had disabilities such as muscular dystrophy or multiple sclerosis. The majority were in my mother's category, where their minds were for the most part alert, but they were physically unable to care for themselves. The activities scheduled were varied, and the nurses and aides were very nice to my mother. She had a roommate and a TV set with remote control, and she enjoyed the Bingo and movies as well as the groups who came weekly to hold Bible studies or just entertain the people. They had a beautician who came in weekly to do their hair, and some of them even married men who were living there.

The home was clean, with beautiful gardens, and my mother enjoyed having us wheel her in her wheelchair outdoors when we visited. We brought her home for all family occasions until she was no longer able to leave because her physical condition had deteriorated so much. (That was during the last months of her life, after she had had a severe heart attack.)

If it is necessary to hospitalize your parent this way, it is important to give your guilt feelings to the Lord. They will come, especially through other people who might say they would never "put away" their parents in that manner. We found the most critical persons to be older people, but we knew that there was no possible way I could care for my mother and see that she had the round-the-clock attention she got in the convalescent home.

It seems only sensible to give a parent the best care possible; it is impossible for the average housewife to maintain her in her home. Either the parent is neglected because of too many responsibilities on the part of the housewife, or else the wife works herself into a nervous breakdown trying to be Superwoman by doing the impossible job of giving round-the-clock care to an ill person while cooking, shopping, cleaning, running errands, and providing care for a family. It is important to be satisfied with the facility in which your parent is installed, and when that is done, leave the rest to the Lord.

What of the parent who is not healthy enough to live alone but not ill enough to be hospitalized in a care center? We know cases of this, and it can be a burden. I realize that in biblical times many members of the same family lived together. However, there were also servants to do the work, and that would certainly solve a lot of the problems which go with communal living. I have one friend whose mother-in-law lives with them and constantly criticizes the meals cooked, the arrangement of the furniture, and the mode of living of the couple and their friends. This woman is not a Christian, which makes the situation doubly difficult. However, in a situation like this we have to remember that God allowed it, that we have something to learn from it, and that when we learn it He may alleviate the problem.

In a family of several grown children, the ideal answer is for each one to bear the burden of the elderly parent for part of the year. However, in some cases where there is an only child, this isn't possible. As always, prayer is a fantastic help, and God can give us the grace for anything, including living with an ailing in-law.

In my opinion, the ideal situation for a woman alone, either widowed or divorced (if she is in good health), is a mobile home park. We know many women who live in adult parks and are delighted with them. They provide both fellowship and security. (Since they are fenced off, there are few cases of intruders.) There are also social activities and recreational facilities. There are potluck dinners, craft classes, sewing bees, and even holiday dinners, for those who are alone and have no other family nearby. There is always a manager on duty in an emergency, and usually he is able to make minor repairs. Most important, mobile homes are usually less expensive than keeping up a house, and there is not the burden of the yardwork. If your parent has a home to sell, it is usually possible to pay cash for the mobile home, with money left over for the proverbial rainy day.

You will find that most elderly people are unduly concerned about money. My mother used to worry each month that her Social Security check would either not arrive or that for some reason the government would decide she couldn't have it. We tried to convince her that we would take care of her even if she didn't have the small check coming in, and that there were no longer "poorhouses" or debtors' prisons, but she continued to worry about it. I found this to be common with most of the others who were at the convalescent home, and also among parents of my friends. Mobile homes are small and compact and easy to care for, but large enough to hold most of the memorabilia that senior citizens hate to part with.

There are also retirement communities for those who are a little better off financially. These are usually groups of condominiums with clubhouses, possibly a golf course, and their own shopping center. There are security guards and many social activities, although they do tend to be a bit more couple-oriented than mobile home parks. There are also church-related retirement complexes. We have at least one in our city, which includes apartments for the individuals with cooking facilities but also provides meals in a dining room for those who do not wish to cook. There are many alternatives to "caring for the elderly and widowed," and all of them should be considered.

If I were alone, I would not enjoy living with any of my married children, even though I love them all and their mates. At my age, the constant chaos of young children would be wearing on my nerves, after so many years of not having babies in my home. It seems wiser to me to encourage the older parent to build a life of his or her own, with worthwhile activities, to travel if he desires and can afford it, and to enjoy a more extensive involvement in church activities. The mature woman has so much to offer in the way of wisdom and teaching. Titus 2:3-5 tells older women to be reverent in the way they live, not to be slanderers or addicted to much wine, but to teach what is good, to train the younger women to love their husbands and children, to be self-controlled and pure, to be busy at home, and to be subject to their husbands.

At our church, the women's Bible study class is set up to take advantage of the teaching of the older women. At the beginning there are prayer and share groups, with leaders, which last for 35 minutes. This is followed by a 45-minute Bible lecture. At the close of the lecture there are elective classes which last for another 35 minutes. These include sessions on marital problems, child care, dealing with teenagers, flower arranging, Chinese cooking, bread-baking, cake-decorating, crafts of all kinds, nutrition, weight loss, exercise, sewing, makeup and clothing style, quilt-making, home-decorating, discussion of the Bible, etc.

Many women are needed as leaders of these various classes, and it is a worthwhile activity for a woman alone to teach in this way. It meets her emotional needs by helping her to feel useful and is certainly helpful to the women taking the classes. We have over 400 women involved, including many from other churches in the area.

I sincerely believe that when we are busy, our health is better. Or maybe it's just that we don't have time to notice those aches and pains that accompany the deteriorating of our bodies as we grow older. Whatever the case, God has plans for us as long as we are on this earth, and if we let Him lead us He will see to it that our lives are always fulfilled and that we are never bored or lonely.

12

Love and A Different Lifestyle

The Live-Together Arrangement

In these changing times, emphasis on marriage has become sadly neglected. Although people are still marrying, the world system seems to encourage LTA—Live-Together Arrangements. Our grandson was watching television the other day while recuperating from a broken toe. As I worked in the kitchen adjacent to the family room, I heard a girl say, "Why do you want to get married? Why not live together first to see if you're compatible?" The program was a popular comedy that is normally seen at prime viewing time in the evening, but this was a daytime rerun. I bounded into the family room and had a talk with Clint about the biblical view of marriage and the way God feels about fornication, although I tried to put it into terms that an 11-year-old would understand.

Eleven-year-olds understand more than I

thought, however. Recently, Clint, his grandpa, and I were doing our regular Monday night Bible study (that we do each week when he spends the night with us), and we were in the Book of Proverbs. It was speaking about the prostitute when Clint asked, "What's a prostitute?" His grandpa and I exchanged glances and I said, "It's a lady who has sexual relations with a man for pay." Clint calmly said, "Oh, you mean a hooker?" We had no idea that he knew what one of those was, but then I realized that there are plenty of them on TV in prime time.

Many parents are troubled and burdened with young people who have chosen the live-together arrangement in lieu of marriage. It is embarrassing, frustrating, and just plain heartbreaking to have our children decide to move in with a person of the opposite sex, with no commitment, and usually with the girl paying half the expenses while giving herself to the guy, no strings attached. This is inconceivable to those of us raised in another generation, where morality was a thing to be proud of and virginity was something we kept until marriage.

Even young people from Christian homes often choose this immoral lifestyle, much to the disappointment of parents who have done their best to be good, moral examples of their children, to train them in Christian values, to see that they attend a good church and Sunday school all their lives, and even to send them to Christian schools. What is the answer?

One thing that we as parents have to face: we can train a child up in the way he should go, but he may deviate from the godly path for a time. We have God's promise that he will return eventually, but meantime much heartache may be in store for us. There comes a time when a child chooses for himself his lifestyle, and we cannot accept the blame if he chooses ungodliness. We are each responsible for our own lives, and if we have done our best as parents, we should not feel not guilty. We all make mistakes, and sometimes we see young people who are the epitome of dedicated Christians coming out of the most ungodly homes possible. Many fine Christian couples have had the experience of seeing one or more of their children reject moral living and turn to sin. There are some things we can do to help the situation, and we will deal with them one at a time.

1. Pray for the young person and the one he is living with.

Much more can be accomplished by prayer than by nagging. The faithful prayers of parents are responsible for more turned-around lives than all the lectures in the world. Pray daily, with your husband or wife, for the wayward child, and trust God to bring him back to the right path of commitment to Him.

2. Let your offsprng know that you are deeply disappointed in him.

Some parents have said to me, "Well, we hate to act disapproving because we don't want to make our son (or daughter) mad at us." I believe that is a risk you have to take. I definitely don't believe in open hostility with them, but making them aware of your disapproval is very necessary.

This can be done in a calm, loving, forthright manner. It needs to be said in words and backed up by actions, so they won't think you've changed your mind and accepted the inevitable.

3. Never allow them to stay together in your home, and never stay in their home with them. By allowing this relationship to exist in your home or by staying in their home with them, you are putting your stamp of approval on it as far as they are concerned. You are saying, "I may not agree, but do your own thing." To condone fornication under your own roof is to agree with it, and it sets a very poor example for the rest of the family, including any grandchildren or nieces and nephews. I would not object to having the couple in my home for a meal, but I would not go to their home unless it was a very special circumstance, such as an illness or if I lived in a different town and was just passing through.

It is a delicate balance between alienating your son (or daughter) and remaining friendly but unable to support the relationship, and only with God's help can this be done. I know it is possible, however, because of having close contact with those in that situation. If you are truly loving at all times, and let them know that although you hate the sin you do not hate them as the sinner, it should be possible to keep your relationship intact.

4. Avoid "preaching" to the couple.

This will definitely turn them off. They know, deep in their hearts, that they are displeasing God, and your saying so only makes them more rebellious. It is odd, but most couples living together like to give the impression that they are married when they are with people they respect. Our daughter worked in a pediatrician's office when she was first married, and a couple with whom she attended high school brought their baby in for a checkup. She noticed from the chart that they were not married and that though the young man was listed as the father, the mother and the baby had the mother's maiden name. They later confirmed that they were living together and that they felt it was "cool," but the mother was wearing a wedding ring!

As the girl extolled the advantages of not being "tied down" to marriage, Nancy was musing to herself on the sad fact that this girl who was condemning marriage was actually very tied down with a baby, but had none of the security of a wife and must secretly have been embarrassed about her predicament or she would not have been wearing a wedding ring under false pretenses.

5. If there are children resulting from the immoral relationship, treat them as you would any grandchildren.

Don't take out your feelings of frustration on the children. Remember, they are innocent parties to the whole situation and did not ask to be born. They need your love and affection more than children of a secure marriage. If you ignore them and the couple marries at a later date, you may not be able to win the confidence and affection of the children at that time. You will also, most certainly, have alienated their mother by your lack of love for her child or children. Be sure that your gifts are equal for each grandchild, including this little one with no legal status. It is possible that you may suffer a deep hurt if the couple breaks up and the mother is not related to you and decides not to see your family again. Love is never given without the possibility of being hurt, and we should not withhold it for this reason. God will provide the grace when we need it, and you can depend upon Him. Trust Him and pray about the situation; He has a miraculous way of resolving even the most difficult problems.

6. Don't be judgmental in your attitude.

It is fine to be on the side of ''right'' and of what God tells us to do in the Bible, but don't ever take the attitude that you would not behave in the same manner if the shoe were on the other foot. We have no idea of the problems and peer pressures our children face today. It is difficult to be the only ''different'' one in high school or college.

One young woman who is a Christian was forced into a very embarrassing situation in a classroom, in which a teacher asked all the students to gather on one side of the room. As he enumerated lifestyles to-day, he asked those who agreed to move to the op-posite side of the room. He started out with adultery and living together, and graduated eventually to those who believed they should be virgins when they married. This girl, a daughter of a pastor, was the only one left on the first side of the room when the teacher finished. She became the object of a lot of laughter, teasing, and derision, but she stood her ground.

How many of us would do the same in a similar

situation at a club to which we belong or among our friends and peers with whom we work? And we are mature people, not high-school children who have a desperate need to be accepted by their fellow students. I believe we would all look back upon our adult years and recall times when we did not stand for Christ or speak out for fear of ridicule.

It was easier to be moral when my generation was young because the other kind of girl was talked about in such a negative manner. Even though there were only a few of them, everyone knew who they were. Nice girls were in the majority and enjoyed the prestige of having a good reputation. In these times, things are turned around—the girls who are immoral are in the majority, and the nice girls are laughed about and don't get invited on many dates.

Even when our daughter was in high school in the late sixties, she sat home quite often even though she was very attractive, because she would not date non-Christian guys and did not drink, smoke, use dope, or do immoral things. Fortunately, she attended a Bible college where she met many Christian guys, and our church grew to a point where there was a college group of well over 200 and there were many dates then.

It is never easy to buck the crowd, and that is what a young person must do today to remain in God's will. Who is to say how many of us would not weaken and fall into sin at a young, impressionable age? Some people have stronger character than others, while some have weaknesses and need more acceptance from their peers. There is an old Indian proverb which says,

"Do not judge your brother until you have walked a mile in his moccasins!" It is well to remember this when you are feeling self-righteous toward your own children.

7. Be ready to either "pick up the pieces" or enjoy the wedding.

If the couple breaks up, it is almost like a divorce. The strong emotional attachment of living together in a marriage situation without benefit of clergy makes it just as hard as if it were a legal relationship when the couples agree to disagree. Usually one person will be the instigator of the breakup, and nearly always it is because he or she has found someone else. Often they have lived together for three to four years and have given of themselves as completely as they would in a marriage, but now one partner is dropped for someone younger who has never lived with anyone. And usually the one who does the breaking off marries the new person.

When this happens, never say, "I told you so." Just be ready to be loving, understanding, unquestioning, and forgiving. Perhaps the Lord will use this to turn him or her back to Himself. This could make your young person ripe to turn to Him and get into a group at church. They feel embarrassed facing their old friends, most of whom were couples like themselves who are living together, and they don't fit in, anyway.

On the other hand, if the whole affair ends happily, with the couple receiving the Lord and choosing wedded bliss, don't mention anything about your unhappiness before—just put all of it behind and be helpful, loving, and excited with them. Remember the parable of the prodigal son and adopt the same "Come home, all is forgiven" attitude of joyfulness that his father did.

8. Really love your child.

No matter what kind of life he is living or how far from the Lord he is, he is still your child, and God gave him to you. In Ephesians 6 God tells us to love our children. He knew there would be times when it would be difficult to do so, or He wouldn't have had to tell us. If you pray for your child every day, you will find it easier to love him, and when you *really* love him with unconditional love, which is the way God loves us, he will respond to it and want to please you. If you have trouble loving your child who has displeased you, ask God to give you His love for your offspring. It is His will that you do this, so you can pray this prayer with complete confidence that it will be answered. Read the parable of the unmerciful servant in Matthew 18:21-35 and see what it says about someone who is unforgiving.

Practice love without having to have the feeling for it, and the feeling will come. All it takes is a step of faith, and you will find yourself loving this wayward child with all your heart and praying for him or her many times each day. This is the answer to that child who has strayed from his heavenly Father and disappointed his earthly parents. There is rarely a spiritual or emotional problem for which love isn't the answer.

13

The Third Generation

The Grandchildren

Most people look forward to being grandparents, and even to that old standard joke that every husband I know has said: "I'm too young to be married to a grandmother!" Grandparents can act silly over the new babies, brag about them, show their pictures, and even spoil them without having to apologize for it. When our oldest grandson, Clint, was about six-years old, one of his mother's friends said, "Your grandma sure spoils you." He replied "That's what Grandmas are for!"

Grandmas *are* for indulging their grandchildren a little but they have some other functions too. They are for reading Bible stories and talking about Jesus; they are for providing those special things that mom and dad can't afford; they are for going to Little League games and dance recitals and *enjoying* them; they are for baking cookies on winter afternoons and not minding the mess; they are for going to the toy store and walking around for an hour without hurrying while a one-dollar toy is chosen; they are for playing games with and losing gracefully (and maybe even on purpose); they are for displaying schoolwork and crafts that are homemade and have mistakes in them, but they leave them on display until the kids are grown up; they are for looking at picture albums with when mommy or daddy was young; they are for giving school pictures to and knowing they'll get hung on the wall or put on the piano for everyone to see; they are for going on vacation with and getting to stay up late and sleep in; they are for making anything you want for breakfast; they are for letting you take a piece out of the cake that's for company before anyone even comes; they are for letting you bang on the piano even when you don't know how to play.

Grandpas have lots of things they do for kids, too—like telling stories, showing how to throw a ball or swim, watching sports with on TV and explaining them, and giving you Certs to eat in church and something to draw on during the sermon. These are just a few of the reasons that kids love to go to their grandparents' homes.

As we mentioned earlier in this book, grandparents have a real responsibility in the spiritual lives of their grandchildren. One of the things we can do is to provide Christian books for them. The Little Arch books, which contain Bible stories in poetry form, are excellent for teaching them the Old Testament stories of David, Jonah, Shadrach, Meshach, and Abednego (and others), and the New Testament stories that Jesus told.

One of the best publications I've seen in recent years is *The Christian Mother Goose Book*. It has all the familiar "Mother Goose" rhymes, but each is rewritten into a Christian context. Humpty Dumpty is put back together by Jesus; Jack and Jill go after "Living Water"; and Jesus finds Little Bo Peep's lost sheep for her. These are rhymes and jingles that all of us know from when we were little children, and to have them remembered with their Christian emphasis is a marvelous idea. Our two-year-old grandson, Jeff, never tires of hearing the rhymes read to him and can repeat many of them already.

Grandma and grandpa also have the responsibility of being good Christian examples to their grandchildren. Sometimes when our own children are grown, we feel we can let down and not be so involved with church, and can be a little more relaxed in the things we say and do, but this is not so. Our grandchildren look to us as close to perfect, which gives us a lot to live up to and a reason for continuing to grow in our faith. They need to see us being faithful in our church attendance, giving, serving, and living our lives as Christ would want us to. Our homes should be comfortable, warm, loving, and peaceful in order to be a good example to these little ones. Our relationships with others should reflect our maturity in Christ, and dissension should be practically nonexistent in our lives. They should be aware of our standards and how we feel about things, and our morals should be above reproach.

Most of all, we should be fun for them to be with. We should care more about them than we do about whether our house gets messed up. (However, we shouldn't let them make a big mess without helping to clean it up; we want to teach them good habits.) We should fill in the places where their parents are too busy, like attending a function to which they are unable to go or helping with homework or reading a story or going shopping at Christmastime, when mom is really rushed

I can remember that when I was a freshman in high school, wooden shoes were very popular. My mother and stepfather thought this was an unnecessary purchase, and they would not help me buy a pair of them. All my friends had them, and at the time it seemed like the most important thing in the world that I should have a pair too. My grandfather came to town and visited us, and I told him how much I wanted a pair of wooden shoes. When he left, he hugged me and put the money for them into my hand. I can still remember how much I appreciated it and how I loved those shoes. There is even a picture of me in my high-school yearbook sitting on the front steps of the school wearing those wooden shoes. I can now appreciate how my grandfather must have felt when he saw me in them, as I have grandchildren of my my own and see them enjoying gifts that I've given them.

Grandparents can provide those little "extras" that mean a lot to kids but are just not in the parent's budget. However, we should be careful not to overcompensate to the point where we are just a ready source of cash and our grandkids take advantage of us. We need to teach them to have a grateful spirit, and we don't do this by giving them every single thing they want, whenever they want it.

One point I must make here is that we must be careful not to play favorites with our grandchildren, any more than we would with our own children. Sometimes there is a tendency to do this as one child responds more to us than the others. One of our son's friends was the apple of his grandmother's eye. He is such a nice, handsome young man and such fun to be with that we can see why she doted on him, but it was almost to the exclusion of the other children in his family. They were really hurt by her favoritism, and I believe that many of their problems as they entered their teens resulted from this.

We have made it a practice that whenever we do something for one grandchild, we do it for all of them. I don't mean that it necessarily has to be done at the same time if they are different ages. We attend Clint's Little League games, but Jeff is too young to be on a team. However, when he and his baby sister, Christy, are old enough, we will support their activities in the same way. We try to spend approximately the same amount on each of them for birthdays and Christmas, and we would never bring a gift for one without including others in the same household. If we are on vacation, we bring back a small souvenir for each one, including Clint's half-sister, Myla. (I am "grandma" to her too because I'm Clint's grandma). We keep these gifts small and relatively inexpensive, realizing that as more grandchildren come along it would be difficult to buy a lavish gift for eight or ten of them.

Not only is it possible to play favorites with giving gifts, but also in the time spent with them. Naturally, you are going to spend more time with those who live near you than with those who don't but be sure to balance out those times fairly evenly between the ones nearby. Our grandson in the same town spends his Mondays with us, but I also drive to another town close by to see our other two grandchildren once a week. As more are added, we may have to double the visits and have more than one at a time, but I don't ever want any of them to feel that I love one more than another.

This brings up the matter of baby-sitting. We need to be cautious in doing this for one of our children more than another. If one couple has two sets of grandparents in the area while one does not, it is inevitable that you are going to be asked more often to sit for the one who does not. This has been our case—our daughter's in-laws are nearly always available to sit for them, since they are not involved with as many activities as my husband and I are. Therefore they see the children more often than we do. In the case of our oldest grandson, his other grandmother is deceased and his grandfather has remarried, so we are much closer to him than he is. This is a result of a circumstance in life which is unavoidable, and it causes no problem in our family. I believe that if we let our children and grandchildren know that we have no "favorites" and that we love them all equally, they will not resent each other's place in our lives. It is the deliberate preference expressed for one child over another that hurts relationships and is devastating to the child.

If possible, it is good to spend individual time with each child. When we lived in the same city as my mother, she did this with our children. She would take just one child overnight and do the things that he or she particularly enjoyed. As our small grandchildren get older, we also intend to do this. It gives us time to get to know the child as an individual and not just as part of a family or half of a brother-sister duo. They are all so different; their interests are not the same, nor are their responses. Their variety of interests and different personalities are what makes it vital for us to spend time alone with each grandchild, pursuing the hobby most interesting to him or her.

One of the most important things we can do as grandparents is to ask God to help us to be flexible and not to get set in our ways and upset when anything gets out of place in our homes. So often older people put their affections on ''things'' to the exclusion of people. Their houses look like museums, with so many china knickknacks around that no child could possibly be there for long without breaking something. They worry about scratches on the furniture and marks on the floor, and then they fret when no one comes over, or if they do, that they do not stay long.

When our children were in high school, our home was a meeting place for all their friends. I especially enjoyed summer vacations because it gave me more time to spend with the kids. The Lord gave me the ability to see them as individuals, not just "kids," and I am glad for all the times we spent just talking. Recently I was teaching a ladies' Bible study and I shared this with them. One of the women said, "I'll bet you had had a lot of damage to your home." I told that I couldn't even remember any damage at all from the kids—only cigarette burns on my furniture by adults. My daughter was in the Bible study and she said, "I think the most traumatic things that ever happened was when one of my brother's boyfriends spilled a glass of Coke on the jigsaw puzzle we were all working, and the ends curled up!" It amused me to hear her say that, as I could remember the incident and how we laughed about it. We treated the young people with respect, affection, and understanding, and they responded in the same way to us.

Recently my brother-in-law found some Bibles belonging to his parents and grandparents in the basement of the home of a relative. He gave them to my husband and me, and inside one belonging to my husband's mother (who died when he was a little boy) was the date she accepted the Lord. It was so precious to us, and it occurred to me what a wonderful idea it would be to write down in our Bibles the dates we accepted Christ and were baptized, and even a little of our testimony for future generations to see. One of the Bibles, given to my husband's grandfather by his father on Christmas eve, 1869, is six generations removed from our own grandchildren. I recently purchased a new Bible to replace my delapidated one, and I wrote as much family information as I thought our future great-grandchildren would want to know. I pray that it will warm their hearts to know that their ancestors loved the Lord.

As grandparents, let us set our affections on those youngsters who will be our heritage when we are gone, and not on material things that we have accumulated during a lifetime. The Bible says, ''Children's children are a crown to the aged'' (Proverbs 17:6 NIV). Let's treat them as we would precious crowns!

14

Evaluation and Survey

The Mother-in-Law Quiz

It would be impossible to write a book that would solve all the in-law problems that ever existed, and I realize that I have barely scratched the surface. I have tried to deal with the most common problems and have given simple answers based on Scripture and my own experience.

It may seem to the reader that there have been no in-law problems in our family, but I assure you that I have been a mother-in-law under the most difficult of circumstances and have learned a great deal over these past 12 years. I have merely been careful not to share anything that would embarrass anyone in my family. Everything I have shared has been proved either in my own life or in that of someone close to me with whose circumstances I am well-acquainted. I pray that what you have read will help you. Though at times it won't be easily applied, with God's help it will work.

The questionnaire following this chapter has been developed to help you understand your relationship to your own mother-in-law, where improvement can be made in your reactions to her, and how you can learn to be the kind of mother-in-law who will be a joy to your children. I have not included a "rate-your-mother-in-law answer sheet" to these questions because I am sure that, after reading them over, you are aware how she rates. If you are a mother-in-law, try to be as honest as you can in discerning how you feel your in-law kids would fill out this questionnaire. Ask the Lord to reveal to you areas where you can improve, and then ask His help in doing so.

My husband has always said that we have invested more time, money, energy, and emotional attachment in our children than in any other area of our lives. If we find ourselves estranged from them as we grow older, our investment has been wasted. Joy in our second half of life depends, to a great extent, upon our relationship with our children and grandchildren. Hopefully, what you have read in this book and applied to your life will make it all that God intended it to be.

The
Mother-in-Law
Quiz

The Mother-in-Law Quiz

1. How is your relationship with your mother-in-law? Very good _____ Good _____ So-So _____ Indifferent _____ Horrible _____ .

2. Is your mother-in-law overly possessive of your mate? Yes _____ No _____ .

3. Does your mother-in-law interfere in your marriage? Yes _____ No _____ .

4. If you had an argument with your mate, would your mother-in-law automatically take his/her side? Yes _____ No _____ .

5. Does your mother-in-law visit too often _____ Just the right amount _____ Rarely _____ Never _____ ?

6. Is your mother-in-law a born-again Christian? Yes _____ No _____ .

7. How would you rate your mother-in-law's marriage on a scale of 1 to 10, 10 being ''great''? _____ .

8. How is your mother-in-law's relationship with her own children? Excellent _____ Average _____ Below average _____ Poor _____ .

9. Does your mother-in-law get along well with her other sons/daughters-in-law? Yes _____ No _____ .

10. How would you rate her overall performance as a mother-in-law on a scale of 1 to 10, 10 being the kind everyone would want? _____ .

11. Does your mother-in-law interfere in the raising and discipline of your children? Yes _____ No _____ .

12. Is your mother-in-law available on short notice to help you out Financially _____ Physically _____ Spiritually _____ Emotionally _____ By baby-sitting _____ ?

13. When she does help you out, does she make you feel Guilty _____ Or grateful _____ ?

14. Does your mother-in-law openly criticize you? Yes _____ No _____ .

15. Do you suspect that your mother-in-law criticizes you behind your back? Yes _____ No _____ .

16. Has your mother-in-law ever caused a problem between you and your husband/wife? Often _____ Rarely _____ Never _____ .

17. Does your mother-in-law relate to your parents Very well _____ Average _____ Below average _____ Poor _____ Not at all _____ ?

18. How does your mother-in-law relate to the parents of her other married children? Very well _____ Average _____ Poor _____ .

19. Are your mother-in-law's standards Very high _____ Average _____ Low _____ Very low _____ ?

20. Do you feel that your mother-in-law is a Blessing _____ or Less than a good influence _____ to your children?

21. Does your mother-in-law encourage your family spiritually? Yes _____ No _____ .

22. Is your mother-in-law basically a tolerant, well-adjusted person? Yes _____ No _____ .

23. Can you get along well with your mother-in-law over an extended visit when you must spend time alone with her? Yes _____ No _____ .

24. Is your mother-in-law fun? Yes _____ No _____ .

25. What would you consider your mother-in-law's basic temperament to be? (Check one or two). Sanguine _____ Choleric _____ Phlegmatic _____ Melancholy _____ .

26. If you had a serious problem, would you go to your mother-in-law for advice? Yes _____ No _____ .

27. Is your mother-in-law a warm, loving, forgiving person _____ or does she tend to be harsh and judgmental _____ ?

28. Is your mother-in-law an outgoing person with many interests? Yes _____ No _____ .

29. Is your mother-in-law overly involved with her own family and their lives? Yes _____ No _____ .

30. Does your mother-in-law often tend to give you unwanted advice or help? Yes _____ No _____ .

31. How would you rate your mother-in-law's walk with the Lord? Mature Christian _____ Spasmodic, up-and-down relationship with the Lord _____ Carnal Christian _____ Seeking for answers _____ Not interested _____ Downright hostile _____ .

32. Does your mother-in-law seem jealous of your relationship with your husband/wife? Yes _____ No _____ .

33. How did your mother-in-law treat you when you were dating your mate? Warm and loving _____ Polite _____ Barely civil _____ Hostile _____ .

34. How did your mother-in-law act during the planning of the wedding? Very helpful & cooperative _____ Overly demanding _____ Resigned but not really happy _____ Wished your husband/wife had married someone else _____ Ignored the whole thing _____ .

35. Does your mother-in-law get her feelings hurt easily, and is she overly sensitive? Yes _____ No _____.

36. Is your mother-in-law overly generous to your family to the point that you feel she takes over _____ Always ready to help to the right degree _____ Seldom senses you have a need _____ Would help if she could but is not financially able _____ couldn't care less if you went bankrupt _____.

37. Is your mother-in-law a burden to you? Yes _____ No _____.

38. Do you enjoy socializing with your mother-in-law? Yes _____ No _____.

39. Would you willingly take your in-laws on vacation with you? Yes _____ No _____.

40. Does your mother-in-law make a sincere effort to please you in birthday and Christmas gifts? Yes _____ No _____.

41. Does your mother-in-law "take over" when she visits? Yes _____ No _____.

42. Does your mother-in-law get along well with people in general? Yes _____ No _____.

43. Is your mother-in-law in good health Yes _____ Nb _____.

44. Does your mother-in-law complain a lot? Yes _____ No _____.

45. Does your mother-in-law play favorites with the grandchildren Always _____ Sometimes _____ Occasionally _____ Rarely _____ Never _____ ?

46. Do you communicate well with your mother-in-law? Yes _____ No _____ .

47. Is your mother-in-law a good friend as well as a relative? Yes _____ No _____ .

48. Do you know for sure that your mother-in-law really loves you? Yes _____ No _____ .

49. If you could choose another person to be your mother-in-law (without changing mates) would you do so? Yes _____ Sometimes _____ No _____ .

50. Are your interests and those of your mother-in-law compatible or similar? Yes _____ No _____ .

51. Can you pray with your mother-in-law? Yes _____ No _____ .

52. Would you like to be the kind of in-law that your mother-in-law has been to you? Yes _____ No _____ .